TURN HIS SEXUAL FANTASY
INTO A STEAMY REALITY

Raise him to the boiling point at the very sight and touch of you. Plunge him into pleasures he never dreamed a woman could give him. Make him want more and more of you—while he gives you more and more and more of what you want.

Remember, when you get together with each other's sensuality, it's even better than he or you ever imagined sex could be. So fling off your inhibitions and follow each step of this unrivaled guide and watch him lust his way into your arms for being so deliciously wicked . . . .

More Ways
to Drive Your Man
Wild in Bed

More
WAYS TO DRIVE YOUR MAN WILD IN BED

GRAHAM MASTERTON

A SIGNET BOOK

NEW AMERICAN LIBRARY

Copyright © 1985 by Graham Masterton

All rights reserved

SIGNET TRADEMARK REG. U.S. PAT. OFF. AND FOREIGN COUNTRIES
REGISTERED TRADEMARK—MARCA REGISTRADA
HECHO EN CHICAGO, U.S.A.

SIGNET, SIGNET CLASSIC, MENTOR, ONYX, PLUME, MERIDIAN
and NAL BOOKS are published by NAL PENGUIN INC.,
1633 Broadway, New York, New York 10019

First Printing, May, 1985

5   6   7   8   9   10   11   12

PRINTED IN THE UNITED STATES OF AMERICA

For Wiescka,
More Than Ever

CONTENTS

Introduction

You are today's woman: feminine, independent, intelligent, outspoken, well-dressed, confident, and very, very ambitious.

You can do a man's job as well as a man; often better. You can meet men and beat them on their own turf when it comes to athletics, music, or art, or repairing a motorcycle.

In the past ten years, you have broken through barrier after barrier of prejudice, unfairness, and downright male hostility. These days, you can be admitted to stock exchanges; run for Vice President; train to be a paratrooper; build your muscles; head up movie companies; fight, run, dance; join the police force; whatever takes your fancy.

But although your social standing in relationship to men may have changed dramatically, *improved* dramatically, how has your sexual standing altered, if at all?

Are you having a better time in bed than women were having ten years ago? Are you more excited, more exciting? Are you more fulfilled? Do you satisfy your mate more? Are you now able to encourage him to satisfy *you* more?

9

Ten years ago I wrote *How to Drive Your Man Wild in Bed*, and ten years ago I spoke to dozens of woman who said that they were dissatisfied with their lovemaking. Not that it was actually *bad*; in some cases it was quite happy and enjoyable. But they always felt that there was something more to be had out of sex . . . something that they were missing.

I wrote the book in order to help them find that "something missing." And thousands of women did. I have a whole shelfful of letters to prove it— warm, provocative, responsive, fascinating letters from women all over the world.

They responded because what I tried to show them was something that no woman could have showed them; that is, what a man expects from you when he goes to bed with you and how you can live up to his expectations. Part of living up to his expectations means training him to give you all the satisfaction that you have the right to expect in return. Good sex is (1) mutual, (2) reciprocal, and (3) escalatory; that is, (1) it's something you do together; (2) it's something you do to each other; and (3) it's something that between you you can build up until you experience the kind of pleasures you thought you would only read about.

Talking to today's more assertive and increasingly independent women, I found a great many changes in your attitudes toward sexual fulfillment. Most but not all of your attitudes are helping you get the pleasure you expect.

You are more *demanding*, without a doubt. You are no longer prepared to let your husband or lover get away with those fumbled, bungled, half-drunken "Saturday night specials." You want more foreplay, very much more foreplay; you want kissing and caressing; and you want *talking*. I know it's difficult for anyone to talk much as they come close to a sexual climax; that would be like trying to recite the Gettysburg Address while sprinting over 800 meters. But even a few gasped-out words of pleasure and passion are better than the stolid silence in which most American lovemaking is conducted. A despairing Jody from San Diego told me, "The only way I can get my husband to shut up talking about football is to say, 'Let's go to bed.' The only time he's quiet is when he's making love."

You are *better informed* about your body. You know more about your sexual parts and how they work. You know more about the physical details of sex. Books such as *How to Drive Your Man Wild in Bed* and scores of explicit magazine articles have at last had a widespread effect on what you know about yourself, and about men, too. One New York secretary admitted, "I always thought men had a kind of narrower pipe inside of their penis which sort of slid up you when you made love. I couldn't imagine when I looked at my boyfriend that I could actually accommodate anything so large as that inside of myself."

You *know more* about lovemaking. Again, informative books and articles have had their effect, as have several important reports on sexuality that have been covered in detail in the media. Television shows portray sexual encounters more frankly and more freely, demonstrating that in ten years public inhibitions about discussing sex have definitely relaxed. You know about orgasms; you know about premature ejaculation; you know something about the more common sexual difficulties such as frigidity and impotence.

You are *less inhibited* about trying new variations in sex, new positions, new locations, and new stimulations. Flavoring your nipples with kirsch and inviting your lover to lick it off for you is no longer regarded as bazarre to contemplate. (In fact, it's probably the best and only way to drink kirsch.) Nor are you so shy about the idea of making love outdoors, down by the lake, amidst the trees, in the back seat of a 747 during the in-flight movie, right on the brink of the Grand Canyon, or in your own backyard.

All of these positive changes in your sexual attitudes make it far easier for you than the woman of ten years ago to become the kind of lover your lover would like you to be, as well as the kind of lover that *you* would like to be.

But there is one attitude that many of today's women tend to have that doesn't help too much, even though overcoming this attitude is one of the keys to a really successful sexual relationship. Over the past ten years, this attitude even seems to have hardened rather than relaxed, and it can so often lead to sexual misunderstandings, resentment, frustration, and aggression between people who could, in fact, become the closest and best of lovers.

The attitude takes the form of a reluctance to discover what your man's deepest sexual desires might be, what unspoken sexual urges he might have. It equally takes the form of an unwillingness to explain clearly and understandably to your man what *your* deepest sexual desires might be.

Part of this reluctance is attributable to shyness and the fear of embarrassment. Suppose you tell him that you want him to stimulate you with his tongue, and he stares at you in shock and surprise? Suppose he tells you that he wants to tie you up to the bed and make love to you while you're lying there helpless? What are you going to say to him if the idea sends shivers down your spine?

Ten years ago this reluctance could be traced to the social feeling that was widely prevalent that the man was the one who was *in charge* of sex; that the man was not only supposed to know everything there was to know about sex, but that he should be able to perform it—from dinner table to bed—with grace, ease, and unfaltering command.

The trouble was, of course, that most men couldn't hack it and should never have been expected to; and those who did were so macho they were laughable. But, of course, there was a whole rash of books for men on *How to Make Love to a Woman* and *How to Get Her into Bed and Satisfy Her for Hours for the Price of a Cheap Meal*, none of which did anything except make most of the men who read them feel even more frustrated and inadequate than they did before.

With increasing equality for women and a greater emphasis on political feminism, communication between the sexes on matters of very personal sexual urges has not improved at all. I asked fifty different men from very different backgrounds what their greatest sexual fear was (among many other questions), and apart from an understandable percentage who were worried that they would not be able to get and keep an erection when they were in bed with a woman whom they wanted to impress, the largest proportion of them admitted that they were anxious about not being able to satisfy their women.

And why were they so concerned about not being able to satisfy their women? Again and again, I was given the answer: "*Because I don't really know what women want.*" And, of course, they were always too embarrassed to ask, especially now that most of you appear to be so confident and so assertive.

You have successfully challenged men on a social and on an economic basis. So naturally many men are subconsciously concerned that you will challenge them on a sexual basis. And if they fail . . .

what's left for them? That's why, to coin a phrase, they have tended to pull their horns in. We see from informal surveys that men appear to have become far more conservative when it comes to sex and far less adventurous; all because they are afraid to put their sexual sensitivity on the line in the face of what they perceive as composed, collected, and sexually demanding women.

In response to this sexual conservatism, however, women tend to have become less open about what *they* want. If your lover appears to be straight as a die and loyal as a Labrador, it becomes all that more difficult to mention the idea of a foursome in a sauna. And many women, however adventurous they are careerwise or in their day-to-day social encounters with men, still expect a man to *know* what he wants out of sex intuitively. In fact, the more independent you become, the more you expect your men to take over when it comes to sex. After a tough day at the office, women feel more than ever like being taken up in Clark Gable's arms and carried up to the bedroom where their every erotic whim will be gorgeously fulfilled.

The trouble is, poor Clark doesn't happen to know what your every erotic whim happens to be; and quite often he's too nervous to ask.

That's why this book is very largely concerned with *sexual communication*—with ways of telling each other and showing each other what you really need. Everything else about you is right: you're fit (or if you're not quite fit, I'll give you some quick tips to make you fitter, especially for the prime purpose of making love); you're positive; you're rightfully pleased with yourself. There is no reason at all why you shouldn't become absolutely the best lover he's ever had. No, more than that—absolutely the best lover he could ever *imagine*.

To reach the point when you can actually change

your sex life in front of your eyes, however, there are many areas of male and female sexuality that we have to explore. We have to look at your physiology, and we have to discuss your feelings. Before you tell your man what you want, before you *show* him what you want, you have to feel confident about what you're going to say. He is probably going to be just as embarrassed as you are; and if you make one comic error, he may very well seize on it and use it as an excuse to defuse the sexual tension. For example, a very pretty young lady from UCLA told me, "I was trying to explain to my boyfriend how to touch my clitoris, how to touch it really delicately, because he used to mash it up and down and around and around so much that it was just irritating. The trouble was, I didn't actually know the proper name for it, and when I was trying to tell him, I called it a 'clitorick,' and he laughed at me so much that I was totally humiliated. I know that he was only trying to cover up for his own failure to please me, but I just wish that I'd known the right word for it, that's all."

You have to know what you're talking about and how to say it. You also have to know how to coax out of the man you love some of his most potent sexual urges—without making him feel embarrassed or that he's somehow compromising himself by telling you about his secret desires and making himself vulnerable to you.

The more masculine you make him feel, remember, the more feminine he'll be able to make *you* feel.

Sex can be a very complex and sometimes frightening experience, even for the most confident women (and men). It involves not only highly skillful physical activity but a whole array of emotions, feelings, and fantasies, quite apart from the overriding politics of male and female sexuality and the personal politics of your particular relationship. How many times, for example, have you made love not just for the affection and the eroticism of it but to display your forgiveness, or to ask for sympathy, or to show that you're sorry, or even to display your aggression?

"Once, I made love to my husband because I was really angry with him; I couldn't fight him so I practically raped him. I suppose I was just trying to show him what power I had over him. I pulled open his pants and rubbed him and massaged him until he was stiff; then I sucked him, actually *sucked* him hard, until he cried out. Then I pushed him back on the bed, and climbed on top of him. I didn't even bother to undress. I simply lifted up my dress, and tugged my panties to one side, and I raped him. When it was over, my anger was all over as well; but both of us were very aware that I had made love to him as an act of rage, rather than an act of love. In the long run, it helped our relationship, because he never repeated the thing that had made me so angry. In the short term, we had a difficult few days. It took a lot of ordinary loving sex to erase the memory of it, and even then it was still there, like a little bit of grit inside an oyster's shell."

That was a 27-year-old Denver woman, an advertising executive, talking about a powerful sexual incident with her husband. To me, it was one of the clearest and frankest examples that I've come across in years of studying and writing about sex of real sexual politics, of sex being used for a purpose other than making babies or pleasuring the participants. Sex is *power*, too, and that adds an extra volatile ingredient into the mix.

Sex is communication; and *communication is the essence of sex.* When you make love to your man you are saying all kinds of things, such as, I love you, I want you, I need you, I respect you, I admire you, I forgive you, I own you, I surrender to you. The physical and emotional messages are many and endlessly varied.

But truly close and ecstatic sex—the kind of sex that will drive your man wild in bed and will also drive *you* wild in bed—can only be achieved if you talk to each other, intelligently and frankly and knowledgeably, so that each of you is aware of the other's needs.

This book, I hope, will help you make love better; but more than anything I hope it will enable you to discuss sex with your man very much better, because out of that discussion will come nearness, and lovingness, and all those fireworks that novelists keep writing about. Great and stimulating sex is within every woman's grasp. The kind of sex that can make you shudder is within *your* grasp, today.

There's one misconception I want to wipe out before we start. And that is that some women are "frigid" or "cold" or "standoffish," or that some of them are "lousy lays." I really hate those words, but I've heard so often from women who have been deserted by their husbands and boyfriends after a terrible argument: "And to cap everything, you were a lousy lay."

When you think about it, calling a woman a "lousy lay" is just about the weakest and most self-defeating accusation in the whole world. Because, as we've already discussed, sex is mutual, reciprocal, and escalatory; and *both* partners are equally responsible for the goodness or the lousiness of what goes on between them. One will coax the other. One may be stronger. One may be more demanding. One may be tired. But terrific sex doesn't mean making love like porn film stars John Holmes and Uschi Digart every single night, three times a night. It means sharing and communicating on a day-to-day basis—making the best of the low spots and yelling out with pleasure at the high spots. It means not being accusatory. It means not so much being selfish but using your own enjoyment creatively to enhance your partner's enjoyment. And that's an idea we'll talk about in much more detail later.

But . . . you know the moment. Just after you've made love and you're lying together in bed, side by side, and you look across at your lover and think: Is he really satisfied? He says I'm the best, the most wonderful woman he's ever been to bed with. But is he telling the truth? Is he really floating on Cloud 109, or is he secretly thinking about Cathy, or Camilla, or whoever his last girlfriend was, or that secretary of his, the one with the tight silky blouse, and how much more exciting and more willing and sexier *she* was?

The trouble is, you don't know how to ask him how good or bad you were. And what's he going to tell you even if you do ask? That you were rigid and unexciting? That your overenthusiasm put him off his stroke? That you handled his penis as if you were rolling out fettucine? That you don't know how to kiss; no, not just *there*, but anywhere?

Unless you've built up a communicative sexual relationship, the only time that a man will ever tell you bedroom truths like these is when your relationship is breaking up. And then he will use them against you like throwing rocks. At the end of a relationship, they all come bursting out; all the petty frustrations, all the little irritations, and then the final condemnation, "And to cap everything, you were a lousy lay."

By then it's usually too late for you to do anything about it, quite apart from the fact that a man who is ignorant and insensitive enough to say that to you is probably best forgotten. But there is always tomorrow; and there are always other men; and there is always the opportunity to improve your sexual talents and, with them, your sexual relationships.

The problem is that it is usually both unsatisfactory and unwise to keep on asking your lover how good you are in bed: It's unsatisfactory because he won't be able to tell you in any helpful or constructive way and unwise because if he *does* tell you, you may find yourself more hurt and more upset by his critique of your lovemaking than you thought you were going to be. Suppose he says, "All right, you asked for it, the fact is that every time we make love you lie there so stiffly." How are you going to feel about making love to him after that? Tense, of course, and nervous, and inadequate, and that's going to make your lovemaking even less successful. Besides, you're going to find that you resent him having called you unresponsive, and who wouldn't?

This is where *I* come in. Because I can explain to you what you may be doing wrong in bed and how you can improve whatever love skills you already possess. I'll tell you how you can make yourself more alluring, more erotic, more of the kind of woman that he fantisizes about. And since there is nothing emotional or explosive between us, I know that you will understand that I am only pointing out some of the areas in which you could improve your loving because I happen to know a lot about it and I want to share it with you. You're a lovely woman. You deserve it.

I can also tell you how you can deal with *his* inhibitions. Because for all of their braggadocio, many men are extremely shy and unsure about sex and what's expected of them. I can tell you how to discover what his secret desires are and how you can go some of the way toward fulfilling them.

I can also make some practical suggestions about what you *shouldn't* do for him. There should always be a bottom line on how submissive and how sexual you're prepared to be. For example, if you don't like the idea of bondage, then he should never expect you to participate. Likewise with group sex, orgies, and sexual variations that are potentially dangerous. That doesn't mean that I'm going to give you *carte blanche* to chicken out of any erotic experience that you're nervous about trying, because to drive your man really wild in bed you're going to have to experiment and at least dip your toe into some of the more unusual sexual experiences. But I'm going to tell you how to say no without upsetting him and without jeopardizing your relationship.

I'm also going to explain to you how you can improve his sexual techinque for him without him feeling that you're being overassertive and unfeminine and without him feeling that you've been critical of his sexual prowess. There is nothing wrong with a man having sexual pride. It's a very strong part of what makes him feel confident and masterly and aroused; and to damage it just for the sake of getting back at him for something is more than spiteful, it's counterproductive. The techniques that I teach to you, you can teach to him, without him even realizing that you're doing it. He'll feel much better for it when he's making love to you, and believe me, so will you.

You will also be teaching him how to communicate his feelings more explicitly; how to tell you what he's fantasizing about without embarrassment and without shame. He needs your help. It isn't any easier for him to tell you that he has daydreams of making love to you when you're wearing Frederick's of Hollywood underwear than it is for you to tell him that you want him to be more romantic, more charming, more positive, more demanding. You would be astonished if you realized how many couples go through twenty or thirty years of sex life together without ever confiding in each other about anything sexual.

One New York librarian said, "She didn't give me head, all those fifteen years of marriage." But wait a minute, I asked him, did you tell her you wanted it? "No, how could I, you don't say things like that to your *wife*." Did you ever give her oral stimulation in order to encourage *her* to do the same for *you*? "She wouldn't have liked it." How do you know she wouldn't have liked it? "I don't know. She just wouldn't. I was married to her for fifteen years, I knew what she was like."

All over the world, every night, young couples and middle-aged couples and old couples lie in bed together thinking separate thoughts, dreaming separate erotic dreams, quite often going through their entire sexually-active lives without ever expressing to any of their partners their innermost wants, their innermost needs, or even their slightest and lightest sexual fancies. And even those who have managed to discuss sex with each other often find that their communication falters when they actually come to try the sexual activities they have discussed.

"I had had an inclination for years to try anal sex with my husband," a 34-year-old college lecturer from Massachusetts told me. "I suppose the idea first entered my mind when we went to see *Last Tango in Paris*—you remember that movie with Marlon Brando and what was her name, Maria Schneider. There was a scene in which they make love on the floor of this empty apartment in Paris; and Marlon Brando uses—butter, I think it was—to make love to her that way. I don't know whether I'm masochistic or something; I don't think so. There was something about the *forcefulness* of it, all mixed up with the romanticism of it, that intrigued me. Then about six years later I was talking to a girlfriend of mine during a workout session, and she said that she and her husband always had sex that way during her period. So it kind of revived my interest, and one evening after I'd drunk a couple of glasses of wine I plucked up the courage and asked my husband if he would try it. We used night cream for a lubricant. I suppose it should have been exciting, and it should have been passionate, but it just didn't work out that way. The more my husband tried to force himself into me, the less he was able to. Well, you know what I mean, he couldn't keep an erection. In the end he got angry and said I was disgusting. That was one of the worst arguments of our whole marriage. Yet I kept saying, you didn't *fail*, my darling; it was the first time ever. Why don't you try it again? But he won't, in case he looks unmanly. And I'm still wondering what it's like, and having erotic thoughts about it; and since I love him, and want to stay with him forever, I don't suppose that I'll ever find out what it's like."

There is another sexual difficulty that is rarely faced by doctors or agony columnists or even professional sexual counselors. It is the simple but sometimes insurmountable realization that sex, like any other physical activity, not only needs courage and a high degree of emotional preparedness to attempt it, but also practice; if at first you don't succeed, you have to go right back to the starting plate and wind yourself up all over again. Anal sex is only one of the variations that requires special skills and experience to achieve with mutual pleasure and staisfaction. Oral sex is just as complicated to the uninitiated. Am I doing this right? Is he bored? Is he feeling anything? What do I do if he comes? What do I do if he *doesn't* come? So are mutual masturbation and any kind of erotic amusement indoors or out.

Most of us still haven't quite gotten the knack

of straightforward missionary-position intercourse, and that's why this book will talk about that, too: without shame, without embarrassment, and without making you feel that you have to be some kind of sexual Wonder Woman, because you don't.

The skills that this book will teach you are concerned with making your sexual relationship closer, and warmer, and more exciting. As the title suggests, they are concerned with making your partner feel happier. But through the ecstasy of your partner, you too will begin to realize the wide range of delicious satisfactions that you deserve. When you've read the last page, and put the book down, and prepared yourself to give the man in your life the time of his life, you'll be able to think with a considerable amount of pleasurable anticipation that you're about to get the time of your life, too.

There's one more thing I want to say before we embark on this journey into sexual self-realization. Sex and sexual predilections are a highly personal affair. Some women who consider themselves quite broadminded can sometimes find themselves shocked or disturbed by some sexual suggestions; other women who seem reserved and quiet can derive the deepest pleasure from sexual behavior that involves the most *outré* of erotic techniques.

I recently met a girl who had appeared in a video production in which she was tied up in leather and rubber and pushed ten-inch needles through her own breasts from one side to the other. Now, even though she insisted that she got a kick out of it, that kind of sex is way beyond the limit. Rewarding sex, as far as I'm concerned, has to be joyous and exciting, and at the end of it, both partners should have not only retained their physical and spiritual integrity, but enhanced it. You should lie there afterward with a *glow*—both of you. No bruises, no blood, no trauma.

But there are people who want to take sex way beyond the boundaries of even the most adventurous of us, and we will discuss these later in the book. What I want to say is that you should *know* about such things and that you should not let them shock you, but that you should personally draw your limits very firmly. Decide what you will happily accept and what you will *not* happily accept.

You can fantasize about the most extraordinary sexual acts. One lady librarian I spoke to in Denver, Colorado, was deeply concerned because she daydreamed about masturbating naked adolescent boys in the middle of a wheat field. She said she had "worse" fantasies—but it took a three-hour interview before she would even admit to *that*. Another woman, from Charleston, South Carolina, told me that she fantasized about having the lips of her vagina pierced and attached to fine chains and having tame canaries flying from the end of each chain.

The point is that *everybody* has sexual fantasies. They are the very stuff of exciting sex. Some women go a long way to fulfilling their fantasies for real, even the cruel and sadistic fantasies. Others go only a little way. How far you are prepared to go is a matter for your own personal predilections and the desires of your partner. You can both arouse a great deal of sexual excitement between you just by discussing your fantasies, even without attempting to act them out. But be reassured (in case you're worried that your man is going to reveal that he wants you to hang upside down from the ceiling tied with ropes) that most men are more than stimulated enough simply by seeing you in stockings and garter belt, or by making love in the great outdoors, or by taking you out to a dinner-party at which he is the only person in the room who knows (apart from you) that you aren't wearing any panties.

Even if you have been married for years and think that you have already squeezed the last drop of pleasure out of sex that you're ever likely to get, you're in for a thrilling, arousing, and ultimately satisfying experience. Because, uniquely, I am going to explain to you now how you can do everything erotic that you ever wanted to, not by being more sexually selfish (as so many feminist sex manuals advocate), nor by being more compromising (as so many traditional sex manuals suggest), but by using *your* desires to fulfill you man's desires and by understanding at last that everything that *you* want out of your sexual relationship can be won by driving *him* wild in bed.

In some ways, I should have titled this book *More Ways to Drive* Yourself *Wild in Bed*—but by the time you have finished reading this book and practicing what you have learned on your lover, he will probably agree that the title is fine as it stands.

I hope you find that this book is an adventure for you, both in mind and in body—an adventure that is not only a pleasure, but that changes your sex life forever.

Graham Masterton
San Diego, 1984

Are You the Best Lover He's Ever Had?

"One evening, John brought home a sex video that one of his friends at work had lent him. It was called *Debbie Does Dallas*. John said it was quite a famous sex movie, and we ought to watch it. Well, I didn't mind at all. I've always liked sex, and I think that I'm pretty open-minded. When we watched it, I was turned on at first, watching all those people making love in the shower and everything like that; but after all I began to feel depressed. I kept thinking to myself: if that's the kind of sex that John wants to see, then maybe he feels that I'm not good enough for him. Maybe, by showing me all these girls having oral sex and things like that, maybe he's trying to make a point, trying to tell me I'm dull. Afterwards, I asked him about it, and he said that I was being ridiculous, but the thought haunted me for a long time, and sometimes it still does."

That was Naomi, a 29-year-old research assistant at MIT. She was talking about a sexual relationship with her husband that had been growing increasingly fractured because of her anxiety about satisfying him and of his inability to reassure her convincingly that she did, if, in fact, she really did.

You see, the problem with sex is that not only is it one of the most difficult physical and emotional activities in which you'll ever participate, it's also the most difficult activity in which to improve your technique. Sex is usually performed in private, in a highly charged emotional environment in which both partners are tense, excited, self-conscious, and intensely concerned about pleasing themselves and each other. It is almost impossible to make an objective assessment of how "good" or "bad" you are in bed, since the experience of even promiscuous lovers is comparatively limited and there is no disinterested third party around to say, "That was a careless bit of caressing there," or "Don't squeeze him so hard," or "Breasts, breasts—don't forget the breasts."

You can improve your squash and your swimming. You can brush up on your French or your shorthand. If you show a talent for any particular activity, you can be taken by expert instruction up to extraordinarily high levels of achievement.

But although sex is one of the most difficult and important of all human activities, it is in its nature that it cannot be taught by third-party coaching. Compare how much more crucial sex is to human happiness than, say, major-league baseball; and then compare how the participants in each activity are trained. What kind of a player would Carney Lansford ever have been if he had been given no more instruction in batting than a book telling him how to hit curves, a few photographs of pitchers winding up, and then a bat and sent out against Kansas City and expected to play like a champion?

Yet, that it is what we expect of ourselves when we have our first experiences of sex. And, since the majority of us are naturally loyal and nonpromiscuous in our sexual relationships (and judging by the latest sociological statistics, we are growing even more so), we acquire very little practical experience before we marry or enter into a long-term or live-in relationship. It is small wonder, when you consider how ill trained and ill informed we are, that so many relationships break down because of sexual tensions and misunderstandings.

Recently, there was an amusing cartoon strip showing a woman filling in one of those *Cosmopolitan*-style "Are You and Your Man Sexually Compatible?" quizzes. The first question was How often do you have sex? She answered, "Practically every night," whereas her husband said "Not often enough." Question two was Do you ever refuse sex with your man? She put down "No," whereas he said, "Yes." After five or six quesitons, she said, "Wow! According to this, we are totally compatible." Her husband responded, wearily, "Imagine that."

The very relevant point that the cartoon was making was that lovers almost always interpret their sexual relationship completely differently, especially when they are too reserved to discuss their desires and feelings with any clarity or detail.

Because there is no training to be had in the techniques and practice of sex, it is almost impossible for you to know how good you are in bed and whether you are pleasing your man at least as much as any other woman he might have slept with, or more.

Of course, the strength of your love and the quality of your friendship make a very big difference. A man will find ordinary straightforward sex with a woman he adores far more satisfying than the most inventive antics with a woman for whom he feels no attraction or respect. But one of the reasons you picked this book up is because you want to be the most exciting lover he ever had or imagines that he ever *will* have.

Linda, from St. Louis, was married for four years to a telephone engineer before she discovered that he was regularly visiting a prostitute. "A girlfriend of mine said that her husband had seen Ray downtown sitting in a car with another woman and that they appeared to be more than just friends; you know, kissing and talking to each other like they knew each other real well. I guess my girlfriend was being spiteful when she told me, but I had to have it out with Ray, and he admitted it straight away and said that he had been seeing this girl, the same girl, for almost eighteen months. I was devastated. I said, 'Why, for God's sake?' And in the end, in a very roundabout kind of a way, it all came out, that he liked a lot of oral sex, and a few other little fetishes besides, which he used to do with the girl he'd been living with before me. Somehow, he said, he'd never felt that he could do things like that with me. He thought I'd be shocked. He said I gave the impression of being wooden and unresponsive in bed, and since I'd never tried out oral sex on him, he thought I didn't like the idea."

And the truth? "The truth was that I didn't really know very much about oral sex. I didn't actually know what to do. I think I'd kissed his penis once or twice, just as a gesture of affection, but I didn't know about putting it into your mouth and licking it and all that kind of thing. My mom had never told me about it, and very few of my girlfriends at school knew very much about boys. I would have done anything to please Ray. I wasn't disgusted by the idea of oral sex, not at all. My only failing as far as I can see was ignorance, but it took me months and months to get over the idea that I was inadequate in bed."

These days, the daughters of more liberated and less inhibited parents are entering their first sexual relationships with a far more comprehensive knowledge of sexual techniques, contraception, and the workings of their own bodies. But even the best-informed girls I have talked to, no matter how aware they are that their boyfriends will need arousing and no matter how eager they are to do it, are not quite sure how they are going to go about it and are often deeply anxious about their ability to compete with other girls.

The questions that I was asked again and again by 16- and 17-year-old girls were "How will I know what to do?" "How will I know if he's satisfied with me?" These questions at first seem to put a very male-dominated complexion on sex; but when you realize that they are exactly the same two questions that young 16- and 17-year-old boys ask me, you can see that we are not talking about innocent young girls subjugating their sexuality to arrogant young boys. They are actually two shy and inexperienced sexes shuffling toward each other in a panic of high desire and sometimes amazing ignorance.

Today's improved sex education and freer discussion about sexual matters has gone a long way toward dispelling among younger people some of the remarkable sexual myths that used to worry their parents:

"I was told that if you let a boy give you a French kiss, putting his tongue into your mouth, you would end up with syphilis and never be able to have babies. I kept my mouth firmly sealed whenever I was out with boys until I was 18, can you believe that? Then I went out with a man of 25 and he told me what nonsense it was."

"My first boyfriend told me that if you turned a man on so that he had an erection, you had to make love to him or else he could be seriously injured internally. I made love to eight different boys before I was 15. In the end I got pregnant, and when I told my doctor what had happened he explained what a fool I'd been.''

"My friends and I always used to think that it was all right to let a boy make love to you if you put an ice cube up yourself afterwards, or washed yourself with very cold water. We thought that the cold would kill the sperm, just like germs. Now that I think about it, it was incredible that none of us actually got pregnant.''

These are just three out of dozens of sexual misconceptions that I have been told by women who reached the age of sexual awakening in the late 1950's and early 1960's. Some of the myths are so strange that it is almost impossible to believe that anybody could think they were true, like the girl who thought if you made love in the moonlight, you would almost certainly get pregnant.

I still meet girls who have been told nothing by their parents about the facts of life and who have had to rely on school gossip, sex-education lessons, and whatever they can glean from occasional articles in magazines like *Cosmopolitan*. Although it's true that there are far fewer girls who know nothing about contraception, there are still many who are completely unprepared for sexual experience and for becoming involved in a sexual encounter that may lead to marriage or a long-term live-in relationship.

Talking to a wide variety of "average" girls—girls from both East and West coasts, as well as the Midwest, the daughters of teachers, automobile workers, farmers, hotel keepers, technicians, etc.—I found that their general knowledge about the basics of sex was reasonably good, certainly much better than it was ten years ago. They knew more about how babies were conceived, as well as how to *prevent* babies from being conceived, and they knew more about their own bodies. They were moderately well acquainted with the intricacies of the male anatomy, although some of them, including those who had regular lovers, were not entirely sure how it all worked. "I know his cock goes stiff but I don't know how. Some kind of muscular thing? Don't ask me. I'm not very good at biology. Is it muscle? Is that it?"

But, as I mentioned in the introduction, there is still a widespread lack of knowledge among women from almost all age groups, all backgrounds, and all walks of life as to what men actually want from them, what men expect when they get into bed together.

"I suppose he just wants to fuck me," said 21-year-old Donna, from Westchester. "I mean—do boys want anything else?" She was talking about the man she hopes to marry and spend the rest of her life with. She knew about oral sex. She knew something about sexual fantasies. She knew about masturbation. But she hardly knew anything about how this knowledge could be applied to give both herself and the boy she loved a full and satisfying sex life.

It was not her fault. Her boyfriend knew just as much and just as little as she did. It is important when discussing sexual matters not to think of placing blame on anybody—men or women or society. It is simply not true to say that men are insensitive to women's sexual needs, or that women are frigid and unresponsive, or that society makes open sexual discussion impossible. Every situation and every sexual relationship is different; and the only possible response to any kind of sexual difficulty is to be constructive and communicative. If fewer women stopped pretending that they were having orgasms, and fewer men stopped feeling ashamed and unmanly because they ejaculated too soon or couldn't keep an erection, and if there were less emphasis on some kind of fictitious "ecstasy," then ecstasy would be very much more of a reality for many more couples—lasting, continuing, ecstasy.

If you begin to have an understanding of what your man wants out of his sex life, what really drives your man wild in bed, then you will at last be able to judge how good a lover you are, at least as far as he's concerned. He may still fantasize about girls he has known before, even while he's actually making love to you, but I will show you how you can use those fantasies to your own advantage and turn him on even more. Fantasies, after all, are only fantasies, and if they are the only competition you've got, then you're not doing too badly. It's when you have to compete against another woman that your sex life is going to get tough; but I have some sound advice on that, too. Sound advice that may help you to keep the man you love.

The very first thing you have to do, no matter how happy or contented your sex life may be, is to try and answer the question that I posed at the very beginning of this chapter: Are you sure that you're the best lover he's ever had?

Don't ask *him* to answer that question. You'll never get an answer that you can be sure is truthful. If he's nuts about you, regardless of your lack of sophistication in bed, he'll say "yes." If he doesn't want to hurt your feelings, he'll say "yes." If he can't think of any other woman that he happens to prefer at that particular moment, he'll say "yes." Take compliments from your lover always, and always take them graciously. But when it comes to matters of sexual satisfaction, trust only what you *feel*, not what you're told. You should never have to ask, "Was it good for you, darling? Did the earth move?" You should be able to sense the answer, even before you ask the question. In fact, if you have to ask the question at all, then the answer is probably "no," or at best, "well, sort of."

"I think the most shattering thing I ever experienced in my whole life was when I read my husband's divorce affidavit," said 31-year-old Kay from New York City. "The woman he was talking about didn't sound like me at all. He made me sound like a frigid, selfish bitch; a woman who never wanted to make love willingly and who never made the slightest effort to satisfy him. I couldn't believe that he had been seeing me through these eyes for all these years. I always thought I was quite good in bed; not a nymphomaniac, perhaps, but quite good, and skillful at making love. But now that I come to think of it, I did always have to wring out of him any kind of compliment about my lovemaking. In retrospect, I believe that I wasn't particularly good. But then I never understood what he really wanted out of sex, and he never told me. If he'd told me, I think I could have made him happy. I think our marriage could have lasted and been very good. That's the lesson I've learned and the lesson that I've applied to all of my subsequent sexual relationships. I never let a man get away with being unsatisfied. And the funny thing about it is that these days I'm never unsatisfied, either. In fact I haven't had so much pleasure in years; or ever."

Kay learned the hard way the basic lesson of communication. It's rarely an easy lesson to learn, because you have to accept right at the very beginning that your love life *does* need improvement, and not too many people, men or women, are happy to admit to that. It always seems more comfortable to gloss over your problems: to put your lover's impotence down to a passing phase; to explain your own lack of excitement as stress, or too much housework, or any other passing family problem. But sex problems have a way of not staying glossed over for very long; they create emotional and physical tensions that affect every part of our lives. The need for frequent sexual communication and communion in most of us is intensely strong; and if either or both partners are not having the satisfaction of being able to communicate and commune at home, then they will very quickly be susceptible to outside enticements.

The answer to the question asked at the opening of this chapter is that you can never really tell for sure whether you are the best lover that your man has ever had—not if you are trying to compete with every woman he has ever known, right from his earliest adolescence. He may have been seduced at the age of 14 by his music teacher; and even if she wasn't a particularly competent lover, she could have made an impression on him that neither time nor you, no matter how adoring and competent you are, will *ever* be able to erase. But then, don't *you* have memories like that? And don't *you* have fantasies of the men you'd like to go to bed with, if only you weren't married or going out with your man of the moment? Lovers have many rights of ownership in law, but they don't own each other's minds, or memories, or dreams, and they shouldn't ever expect to.

No—where you can prove yourself to be the best lover he's ever had is by simply being terrific in bed: sparkling, erotic, frank, receptive, creative, experimental, and always ready to understand his needs. You may never be able to override his memories and his fantasies, but you will be able to make sure that he is quite content to leave them as they are, as memories and as fantasies. And no matter how they irk you on occasion, you will always have to admit that nobody has any right to be jealous, either of memories or fantasies, provided memories stay in the past and fantasies remain in the future.

"Jack was always talking about a girl he had dated when he was 19, a girl called Susan, a young trainee teacher. The way he talked about her, you would have thought she was the most beautiful girl in the world: big blue eyes, lovely long legs, big breasts. I couldn't help it, I always used to start feeling jealous when he talked about her. Then one day I was walking across the university campus and I saw a young man of about 20 who was really eye-catching. Very handsome, curly hair, a strong physique, and I thought how attractive he was; but at the same time, how *young* he was, and how I could never be bothered to have any kind of an affair with a boy of that age. I might have dreams about it, going to bed with a boy like that. But he wasn't what I wanted; and I realized then that Susan for Jack was only a dream, a memory of some time long ago when he was pleased and happy and excited.

"I understood that if there was no harm in me looking at that young boy and having sexual thoughts about him—even if I thought about making love to him, about his prick and his balls and his naked body, and I knew there was no harm in *that*, no betrayal of Jack or of anything that we meant to each other—then there couldn't possibly be any harm in Jack musing about his Susan. In an odd way, he was almost paying me a compliment, telling me that once he had loved a girl as beautiful as this, but that now he loved me more. I went back home that day and as soon as Jack came into the door I demanded that he take me upstairs to bed and make love to me, and I wouldn't let him go until he'd done it three times."

That was Jacqueline, a 28-year-old postgraduate lecturer at the University of Wisconsin. Her sudden insight into her husband's sexual memories proved to be the catalyst for an improvement in her sex life and in her relationship with her husband as a whole, which, she confided, "was the making of us, as a happily married couple."

Not all improvements in a couple's sex life come so dramatically or so quickly. Remember that I said that sex is a complicated skill that you are expected to acquire without being coached and with nobody to help you but your partner, who may often be as ignorant and as ill equipped to deal with anything so elaborate and so stressful as sex as you are. Never believe what you read in romantic novels about men being "consummate lovers." They're not. None of them. Not even the handsomest, most considerate, most athletic of them. That's why, if you know all the fundamentals of responsive sex and how to share your knowledge with him, you will unquestionably be the best lover that your man ever came across, or is ever likely to. And believe me, he'll know it.

Here's a questionnaire that may help you assess what you need to do in order to become your lover's greatest lover. Answer it as truthfully as you can (on a separate piece of paper, if you prefer, where your husband or friend won't find it).

1. I know just what my lover's strongest sexual prefererence is—YES/NO.
2. When we go to bed together, I often take the initiative in making love—YES/NO.
3. My lover and I have frequently discussed our sexual fantasies—YES/NO.
4. If he asked me to, I would act out any of my lover's sexual fantasies—YES/NO.
5. I would consider using pornography to enhance our sexual excitement—YES/NO.
6. When my lover pays obvious attention to another woman, I try to see what it is that he sees in her—YES/NO.

7. I would consider dressing in a special way in order to excite my man—YES/NO.

8. I have described to my lover how I particularly like to be stimulated—YES/NO.

9. Nothing that my man and I could do together sexually would upset me or make me feel ashamed—YES/NO.

10. My lover is the first person I turn to when I feel upset or angry or when I need help—YES/NO.

11. I know all about my lover's previous sex life—YES/NO.

12. If my lover did not satisfy me when making love I would tell him—YES/NO.

13. I would like it if my lover made love to me in different locations, such as someplace outdoors—YES/NO.

14. My lover and I have worked out a mutually satisfactory method of contraception between us—YES/NO.

15. I would masturbate in front of my lover—YES /NO.

16. I do not believe that my man has any sexual inclinations that he is keeping secret from me—YES/NO.

17. I have no sexual desires that I am keeping secret from my lover—YES/NO.

18. I would happily consider giving my lover sexual surprises, such as greeting him in the nude when he comes home—YES/NO.

19. If I could learn new ways of exciting my lover, I would be very interested in them—YES/NO.

20. I would like to watch my lover masturbating in front of me—YES/NO.

To work out your rating in this questionnaire,

award yourself two points for every yes answer and one point for every no answer.

If you scored 30 or more, you are a very open-minded, sexually creative lady who is more than ready to improve her love life beyond anything that you have imagined before. If you scored 20 or more, you are sexually balanced, very liberated, and are the kind of lover that any man would be pleased to take to bed (or anywhere else). If you are particularly hard working when it comes to improving your sexuality, you will probably become the most exciting lover that your man has ever come across.

If you scored less than 20, you're reticent, aren't you? You're shy about sex, and a little lacking in confidence? But you have no need to worry, because if you read this book and learn whatever it has to teach you, you will undoubtedly blossom into an incomparable lover. And you know what they say—those ladies who start off by being shy are very often the most energetic and dynamic lovers once their inhibitions have been released. So behind that caution and modesty, there's a sexual firecracker waiting to be lit, and that's you.

Questionnaires like these can be a genuine help when they provoke you into thinking what your attitudes toward love and sex really are. They can never provide you with a conclusive personality profile, even when they are 200 questions long and cover every single sexual subject you can think of. But if your responses to these twenty questions have been more positive than negative, your attitude toward enhancing your sex life is already open, and all you need now is the knowledge and the technique to improve it beyond measure. Even if you haven't yet done any of the sexually positive things mentioned in the questions; even if you haven't yet discussed your sexual fantasies with your lover, or masturbated in front of him, or taken the initiative in bed, but you feel that you could happily do them, given the means and the encouragement, then you, too, are equally ready for the great adventure of more wildness in bed.

And even if you haven't been able to answer yes to more than a very few questions, and you still feel very nervous and reserved about trying any of the activities mentioned in them; if you recoil at the thought of pornography, if you wouldn't make love outside of your bedroom for all the oranges in California, and if you would never go to a party without your panties, you should still read on because you will find plenty of good reasons why you should at least consider acting a little more erotically and plenty of reassurance that you won't be acting immorally or loosely and that you won't lose your femininity or your dignity.

Sexual love has a dignity all of its own, as those who have achieved the very heights of ecstasy know. Whatever you happily do to reach that ecstasy is also invested with the same quality.

This is Rosie, a 26-year-old college wife from the University of Wisconsin. She's a modest girl brought up in modest surroundings by very conservative parents. Yet, with the encouragement of her husband Daniel, she found a new sexual ecstasy that added excitement to her sex life for ever afterward.

"We were on vacation in Southern California, and one morning we both woke up very early, around six o'clock, and went for a walk on the beach. There was nobody around for miles, only the seagulls and the surf. Daniel paused, and kissed me, and then he slipped his hand inside my shirt and started caressing my breast and stiffening my nipple. I tugged away from him, half-playfully but also embarrassed, and started running along the beach. He caught up with me beneath some rocks, and laid me down on the sand. I knew what he wanted to do, and I said no. We'd never made love in the open air before. You tend not to where we come from, near Sheboygan, because it's not often warm enough, and folks don't really do that kind of thing, at least not the folks that I know. But Daniel said, 'Pretend you're in a movie. Pretend it's just a dream.' And, you know, I managed to do that, and I stopped being tensed up and anxious, and I let him take off my shorts and my panties, and when he started stroking my thighs and caressing me between my legs, I closed my eyes and allowed myself to enjoy every minute of it. After a while he started to rub me with his fingers, and then slip his fingers inside of me, and I opened my legs wide, and I could feel not only his fingers but the wind playing between my thighs, and the sensation of that was like nothing I'd ever felt before. As he excited me, I began to feel even less inhibited, and I began to fantasize that maybe somebody was watching us make love from somewhere up on the cliffs, and instead of making me worried, like it had before, it made me even more excited. At last I was so aroused that I grasped Daniel's cock with both hands, and raised my legs up in the air and guided him into me. We made love as if we were both going crazy. We hadn't made love like that in six years of marriage. I was almost completely out of control.

All I could think of was the feeling inside me, and the incredible sensation of being on the beach, in the open air, fucking my husband where anyone could have come by and seen us. I climaxed first. I hadn't had a climax like it for a long time. In fact it was probably the most earthshaking climax I'd ever had. Then I felt Daniel shaking, and his come flooding inside of me, and I lay back and opened my eyes and all I could see was the sky and the cliffs, and all I could hear was the surf, and all I could feel was tremendous contentment. After that, we often made love outdoors. Once, we even made it in midwinter, in the snow. It gives your nerve endings a new kind of sensitivity that you never get to feel when you stay in your bedroom all the time. It makes your nerves jangle! I mean, why do people like to eat out of doors? There's something about it that improves the taste. And when I think how shy I used to be— when I think that two years ago, if somebody had suggested I'd be enjoying something like that, I'd have stared at them as if they were out of their minds . . . well, all I can say is that you can live and you can learn."

Here's Daphne, a 32-year-old housewife from Long Island, who wrote to me soon after the publication of *How to Drive Your Man Wild in Bed*. "I had never bought any kind of book about sex before, and I went into the bookstore four or five times before I eventually plucked up the courage to buy yours. I was even foolish enough to tell the girl behind the counter that I was buying it for a friend, and that *I* certainly didn't need anything like that. But the trouble was that my sex life at that time was almost nonexistent. Gordon and I scarcely made love at all, maybe two or three times a month, and even then I felt that he was only doing it to relieve the physical pressure on himself, and not because he wanted to show me that he loved me. I felt that a whole lot of the trouble was my fault, that I wasn't exciting enough for him. I remember when we first married he was always talking about his old girlfriends, and I began to believe that I was a disappointment to him by comparison. I began to think that every other woman was sexier and more attractive than me. Then I read your book and it suggested oral sex which we had never done. It really hadn't even occurred to me to try it; and Gordon had never done it to me.

"I suppose when I come to think of it now he was as ignorant about sex as I was, but of course you're not supposed to say things like that to a man; well, I wouldn't have said it to Gordon, he would have been hurt and angry both. Anyway one morning he was lying in bed and I slipped down the bed and opened up his pajamas and started to massage his penis. I could feel him waking up, and I wondered what on earth he would think, but he lay there not saying anything, and it was only a moment before his penis started to rise, until it was really hard. There was a moment when I nearly chickened out, but then I kissed the top of his penis, and ran my tongue around it, and stuck the tip of my tongue into the little cleft in it; then I took the whole head of his penis into my mouth and began gently to move my lips up and down, while my tongue continued to flick at him, just the way you said. I believe he was shocked at first, we'd never done anything like it before, although he never admitted afterwards that it came as a surprise.

"I found that it was exciting me, having my mouth filled up with his penis, and I began to stimulate him with my tongue more and more quickly, and also to rub the shaft of his penis with my hand. I was so excited in fact I put my other hand down between my legs and started to diddle myself, and the panties of my baby-doll pajamas were soaking. Then he suddenly said, 'My God, Daphne, you're fantastic,' and he ran his fingers into my hair, and held my head with such tenderness and gentleness. Then he suddenly said, 'I'm coming,' and he tried to draw his penis out of my mouth, but I wouldn't let him, I knew from what I'd read in your book that I wanted to swallow his come; and when he realized what I was going to do he came straight away. I was so excited that I came to, and swallowed everything, and licked and sucked him afterwards to make sure that I'd taken every single drop. It sounds like one of those Harold Robbins books when I talk about it now; very lewd. Perhaps it was, in comparison with what we'd been doing before. But it woke up Gordon's interest in me, not only in bed but all the time. When we went out together, he became much more courteous and possessive. He began to bring me gifts. It changed everything; and we've never looked back. I think we learned to fall in love with each other, to be honest with each other both sexually and emotionally; and I realized that we'd never really been in love before.''

If you scored very high marks in our questionnaire, then you can say to yourself with some certainty that you're the best lover your man has ever had. If you scored low marks, but you're eager to change so that you can come back to the questionnaire in a week or a month and score 100 percent, then you're about to become the best lover he's ever had. Either way, you're a winner.

2

Exploring Your Magical Vagina

The very word "vagina" is negative. It comes from the Latin, meaning the sheath of a sword, and was originally coined by the Romans as a ribald joke. "Vagina" gained respectability, however, as anatomists came to consider it the most apt description of what they regarded as a tube that joined a woman's external sexual organs with her womb.

Many men and many women still regard the vagina as nothing more than a "hole," as you can see from the way it is described in erotic and pornographic fiction. Picking up two men's magazines, both of which are freely available on newsstands, I can read without even searching for the word, "Sam nodded back and then started to ease that monster cock of his into my cunt hole," and "Even more sperm than I imagined one man could have went inside my hole."

In the past two decades, however, your vagina has been gradually recognized as an organ just as magical and just as complicated as your lover's penis; in fact, in many ways it is much *more* versatile. Just because it happens to be internal rather than dangling around outside, that doesn't mean that it isn't beautiful and positive and that it doesn't have a shape and a form and an esthetic quality all of its own.

What we have to do together now is explore your sexual organs so that you get to know them and how they perform with the greatest possible intimacy and in the greatest possible detail. In the past decade, there have been some extraordinary advances made in the scientific examination of the vagina, including the use of full-color motion-picture cameras inserted into the vaginal barrel (as scientists rather unromantically call it) during the very moment of orgasm. Many myths and misunderstandings have been dispelled, and it has been clearly seen that the vagina is an extraordinary part of a woman's body: sensitive, receptive, and instantly responsive.

I want you to think about your vagina as a shape in itself; a shape that changes when you become sexually aroused, just as the shape of a man's penis changes. You never think of your mouth as being negative, so why should you think of your vagina that way? Especially when it is such an independent, flexible organ, capable of giving such pleasure both to you and to the man you love.

It is also vital that your lover get to know your body just as closely as you do, and that is why I am going to encourage you, first, to read this chapter carefully on your own, exploring yourself as you do so, and afterward to go through the chapter with your lover, involving his fingers in the touching and discovering process while you read the words out loud.

Touching and discovering between sexual partners is an essential part of developing that intensely close physical bonding that can make it possible for you to take your lovemaking far beyond the normal experience with which most couples have to be content. You can never make a vase in pottery without having the experience of handling the clay and operating the wheel; you can never knit, or sew, or dismantle an automobile engine without feeling and investigating the parts both intellectually and with your finger tips. Equally, you can never expect to be good in bed without both of you exploring each other's bodies and getting to know how they feel and how they work.

You may feel reluctant to let your lover touch you. Laura did. She's a 29-year-old advertising space seller from New York City, elegant, groomed, and sometimes, by her own admission, haughty. "My body is my own," she told me. "I'm an independent woman. I wouldn't allow any man, even a man I loved, to explore me as if I were some kind of anatomical experiment." But suppose he was just interested in seeing and feeling how your body reacted? "I don't date high school boys; the men who take me out should know all about a woman's anatomy already." But suppose they don't—as many men don't? "Then, tough." Not even if one of them encourages you to do the same to him in return? "I want love from my lovers, not lessons."

Laura's sense of feminine independence was understandable; but it was depriving her of the pleasure of being touched and explored by men who cared for her; an experience that can be as exciting as it is informative. She was also depriving herself of the opportunity to learn more about her lover's sexual organs and of finding out exactly what it is that excites him the most.

There is room in successful lovemaking for pride, selfishness, self-indulgence, even arrogance. But there is no room for reticence or for any refusal to share what you have and what you are. When you make love, you are using your body to express your femininity; you are giving yourself to the man you love, the man who arouses you. Anything that you hold back from him will only reduce your own enjoyment and ultimately the quality of your sexual relationship. So—even if it doesn't come naturally to you, even if you have to make a concentrated effort—allow him to investigate your body as if he had never seen a woman's body before.

You may think that the idea of doing this is absurd, especially for adults who have been making love for years. But let me ask you this: Could you sketch a diagram of your lover's sexual organs, naming every part of them, what they do, and how sensitive each part is in relation to other parts? Do you happen to know exactly which way your lover prefers you to grasp his penis when you're arousing him? How fast he likes you to rub him? Do you have any idea of how he feels when he's approaching climax, or what you can do either to speed it up or to delay it? Have you ever explored his body with him so that he can tell you?

You may be the exception, but 90 percent of the women I spoke to when preparing this book said, "No," they had never touched their lover's sexual organs for the specific purpose of finding out how they worked and what it felt like when they were making love. In other words, sexual communication between consenting adults fails right from the very beginning. They don't even know what their partners feel, or how their sexual organs work, or what they can do to improve the sensation. And they don't seem to feel any particular urgency to find out either.

In the bar of a very well-known Los Angeles hotel I asked ten different men—all of them well-dressed, sophisticated-looking types—if they happened to know what a woman's sexual organs actually looked like and if they would draw me a diagram to illustrate them. These weren't adolescent boys; these were grown-up, successful, well-educated men, one of whom admitted to having been married three times. Yet the drawings they submitted as their idea of what a woman's sexual organs looked like were—not to be too unkind about it—laughable. Three of them drew nothing but a bushy slit, although one of them had included the legend "clitoris" and "vagina," missing both locations by inches. The rest of them produced fanciful drawings that might have been considered adequate portrayals of a city traffic system but were nothing at all like a woman's sexual organs.

I asked eight women to draw me a similar diagram, and only one of those diagrams was any more accurate than the ones supplied by the men. "I've never examined myself, not closely," said a 22-year-old art student from Charleston, South Carolina. "I don't think that examining yourself is relevant to having a happy sex life." Did she herself have a happy sex life? "Not particularly. I suppose I'm just old-fashioned and rather modest."

Knowing your sexual organs is important. It helps you to understand yourself and your physical responses; it helps to dispel undue shyness about them; it helps with sexual hygiene; and more than anything else it helps to reassure you that you are normal and healthy and that the physical changes that you can observe in yourself during sexual arousal are the same physical changes that every woman undergoes.

To examine yourself, on your own, choose a time of day when you know that you are not going to be interrupted. Take the phone off the hook if you have to. Lock your door and draw your blinds. It should be done at a time when you need think only about yourself, in silence, and with respect for the magical body that you possess. Revere your vagina. You are made in the most incredible way. Take one hour out of one day to appreciate how beautiful you are. It is the most fitting gesture you could make to show that you respect your femininity and that you are serious about improving your sex life.

Take off all of your clothes, and sit on the bed or sofa with all the lights on and a good clear mirror. Have a flashlight beside you if you want to; there is nothing indecent about looking as deeply as you can into your own body.

It isn't a bad idea to have a glass of wine beside you to help you to feel that this is really a special occasion.

Your external sex organs are usually referred to as your *vulva*. If you sit cross legged, the outer lips of your vulva, the *labia majora*, will open naturally, revealing the pink inner lips, the *labia minora*. Usually, except when you are parting your legs, as you are now, or when you are making love, the *labia minora* will close together, protecting your vagina and your urethra.

Some women have very large vaginal lips; others have smaller ones. Some men have sexual preferences about large or small lips, but not very many men do. The size of your labia makes no difference to your sexual capacity in any way. One of the advantages of today's more relaxed attitude toward pornographic photos is that you can compare the appearance of your vulva with those of other women. If you have seen only a very few men's magazines, you will have realized by now that vulvas come in all shades and shapes and sizes and they're as varied as the faces of the women they belong to; but essentially they all have the same component parts and essentially they are all beautiful.

"My mother is a very free-minded and sensible woman," I was told by 22-year-old Annabel, from Darien, Connecticut. "When I was thirteen, and just reaching puberty, she remained as open about letting me see her naked as she had done when I was small. One evening after we had played squash together, we went to her bathroom and took a shower together. She soaped me and washed me, and then she let me do the same to her, feeling her breasts and her body as much as I wanted to. Then afterwards, when we were dry, we went into the bedroom and she gave me some of her perfume, and we sat together naked on the bed and she showed me her vagina, explaining everything that she knew about it, and how it felt when she caressed it. She explained that she had masturbated as a girl, and that it was perfectly normal, and that if I wanted to do it there was nothing in it but pleasure. I realize that not all mothers would feel comfortable about letting their daughters touch and explore their vaginas, but for me it was a very close and re-assuring experience."

Where your labia minora meet at the top, they form a hood (or a prepuce) over your clitoris. In some women, this hood meets below the clitoris, too, forming a frenulum.

Your clitoris is the most important part of your sexual anatomy—in fact the very name of it is a clue to how important it is. The word "clitoris" comes from the Greek word *kleitoris*, meaning key; and this is exactly what it is, the key to your sexual enjoyment and to that of the men you love.

Only a very small part of your clitoris is actually visible, although again there are minor variations from one woman to another. What you will probably see is a small pink button about a quarter of an inch in diameter; but if you feel beneath the skin just above this button you will be able to make out the shaft of the clitoris itself, which is formed by two closely connected segments of tissue, which can be large or small, without having any noticeable relevance to a woman's sexuality, but which are usually about an inch long.

In many ways, these tissues that form your clitoral organ are similar to the tissue that makes up the male penis. When you become sexually excited, they can become engorged with blood and swell in size, although the clitoris never actually becomes erect, like a penis. The two segments of tissue are joined to your pelvis on either side of your vagina and are controlled by muscles that can contract to prevent blood from escaping from them, in a similar way that the muscles in a man's penis tighten to prevent blood leaving *his* swollen tissue.

There is another muscle underneath the clitoral shaft that is similar to the muscle that shoots your lover's semen out of his penis when he reaches a climax. This muscle divides into two as it runs downward from the clitoral shaft and encircles your vagina. When you reach an orgasm it rhythmically contracts, just as the muscle in your lover's penis contracts, and gives you those highly pleasurable sensations of uncontrollable spasm.

Your clitoris responds much more slowly to erotic stimulation than your lover's penis, however. It will only begin to enlarge after your vagina has begun to secrete lubricating juices and you are already in quite a high state of sexual readiness.

There are dozens of incredible myths about the clitoris, many of which have been perpetuated by modern-day sexologists and that I still see repeated time and time again in so-called "authoritative" books on sexual instruction. You can usually sniff out a sexual myth just by using plain common sense and by the way in which they include some moral or sexually political ingredient.

For instance, take the myth about clitoral and vaginal orgasms. For decades, it was thought that there were two kinds of orgasm. If a woman achieved orgasm through touching or rubbing her clitoris, the myth suggested that the quality of the orgasm was somehow inferior to the one that could be achieved by the penetration of the penis into the vagina. Vaginal orgasms were often more difficult to reach, said the myth, but they were very much deeper and more fulfilling. Even some extremely reputable sex researchers said that very early sexual experience would lead a girl to have only clitoral orgasms and that she would need long and intensive training by the man in her life to make it possible for her to have those deep, fulfilling vaginal orgasms.

Of course, the whole idea of two kinds of orgasm is complete nonsense. Different orgasms achieved at different times by different means under different circumstances or with different men may certainly feel different. They can vary from a small shudder to a hip-threshing, vulva-twitching, tongue-biting, screaming, wonderful explosion. But men experience just as much variety in the quality of their climaxes, and nobody ever talks about penile orgasms versus testicular orgasms.

Some women are capable of achieving orgasm simply by massaging their breasts, but like women who reach climaxes by rubbing their clitorises, or by sexual intercourse with a man, or by any other means, they go through the same rhythmic contraction of the muscle around the vagina.

When you eventually ask your man to discover your sexual organs with you, you will be placing a very great deal of emphasis on the way in which he should stimulate your clitoris. He should know that it is *highly* sensitive because it has a wealth of nerve fibers in it that carry signals of pleasure or irritation directly to your brain. Tell him that among these fibers there are corpuscles that are incredibly responsive to being touched—the technical name for them is Pacinian corpuscles, but it will be simpler if you tell him they are like sensors.

As you show him your clitoris, you will have to explain to him that it is *not* like a miniature penis and that it behaves very differently from a penis in a number of ways that he must understand if he is going to be the kind of lover you really adore.

Tell him that most women, when they masturbate, do not rub or squeeze the clitoris itself, not directly, but apply pressure to it by touching the surrounding vaginal area. Show him how you masturbate. Every woman masturbates differently: Some use the very lightest of touches; others press their thighs together tightly, others like to run their finger tips up and down their inner lips and penetrate their vaginas. Let him see how much your clitoris swells as you masturbate and become sexually excited.

Sexual research has shown that some women's clitorises enlarge to nearly twice their normal size; others scarcely enlarge at all.

As you begin the slow buildup toward orgasm your clitoris tip will begin to withdraw under the prepuce until it can scarcely be seen or felt if your man is stroking it directly. Many men, not understanding that this is a signal that orgasm is approaching, stop stimulating their lovers at this point; and as you probably know from experience, this can be *extremely* frustrating.

Show him that you can achieve orgasm after your clitoris has withdrawn as long as the surrounding area continues to be stroked and caressed. The withdrawal of the clitoris shows how mistaken it is to believe that direct and continuous clitoral stimulation is a requirement for satisfactory lovemaking. And this, in turn, shows how wrong it is to believe that the size or prominence of your clitoris makes the slightest difference to your sexual responsiveness. Women whose clitorises appear to be very small or hidden high up under the hood of their labia minora are just as capable of achieving ecstatic orgasms as women with prominent clitorises.

During intercourse, it is the way that your lover's penis rhythmically tugs on the muscles surrounding your vagina (a tugging that of course is transmitted through the muscles and the nerve fibers to your clitoris) that gives you all of the pleasure and all of the fun. Direct stimulation may sometimes be desirable and enjoyable, but it isn't essential.

Twenty-six-year-old Joy, from Sherman Oaks, California, told me about the special way in which her lover Philip stimulated her clitoris and vulva—a technique that worked especially well at times when *he* had reached a climax and *she* hadn't quite made it.

"I lie back on the bed or the couch or wherever we happen to be making love, and Philip kneels between my open legs, and massages his stiff cock against my thighs, and against my stomach, and sometimes he kind of wraps my pubic hair around it. Then he uses his cock to massage my clitoris, rubbing the head of it up and down between my legs so that my clitoris slides up and down the groove in his cock, you know? And it fits perfectly, and the feeling is sensational, particularly when he starts to get juicy and that juice lubricates my clitoris. The temptation actually to start making love is very strong, but we see how long we can go on like this before Philip has to push himself into me. He rubs his cockhead all around the outside of my cunt, sometimes putting it in just a little way, not too far, and tugging it from side to side. Then he starts massaging my clitoris again, quicker and quicker. Sometimes I've reached my first climax even before we've started actual intercourse. Other times, he has, too, but that can be just as fantastic, because he ejaculates all over my clitoris and between my legs, and then he massages me with his fingers, very quickly and very lightly, using his semen as a lubricant. By the time I climax, he's usually ready again, and so I get the best of both worlds."

The so-called "G-spot," which when stimulated is infallibly supposed to bring on orgasms, is nothing more than the nearest location inside your vagina to the underside of your buried clitoral tissues. Stimulating that spot is bound to be highly pleasurable since it gives you that good, indirect arousal—arousing but not irritating.

While you are sitting on your bed, examining your vulva in your mirror, gently draw back the hood that covers your clitoris tip so that you can examine it more closely. Then gently start to masturbate yourself so that you can watch exactly what finger movements you make to stimulate yourself the most. Watch carefully because the time is going to come when you will want to explain and demonstrate these finger movements to your lover.

Do you actually touch the tip of the clitoris itself? Do you stroke the shaft of it? Do you press on it, beneath the skin? Some women like to apply a gentle rhythmical pressure to the pubic mound above the vulva; others prefer to stroke the lips around the vagina.

As you masturbate, watch carefully how your vulva changes in color and appearance. If you feel like bringing yourself to orgasm now, by all means do so; but if you would prefer to wait until you finish your full exploration, then we'll continue.

If you reach a satisfying climax when you make love, your clitoris will quickly return to its normal exposed position and the blood will empty out of your clitoral tissues, leaving you with a feeling of relief and relaxation. If you reach a high pitch of arousal, however, and do not have a satisfactory orgasm, your clitoral tissues will remain congested with blood, and that is what causes the intense physical frustration you feel. The only answer: Turn back to your man and encourage him to give you that orgasm you failed to reach before.

Henrietta, a 30-year-old grade-school teacher from Albany, New York, said, "I went through five years of marriage with Douglas without ever reaching a climax once. My mother had never told me about climaxes, and the only climaxes that I had ever experienced were during masturbation; and because they were experienced during masturbation, naturally I thought that they were wrong and immoral. Then one day I was having coffee with a rather outspoken friend of mine from school, and she said quite matter-of-factly that whenever her husband was away on a business trip she used to masturbate. 'I couldn't live for two weeks without at least *one* orgasm,' she said. Well, we started talking about orgasms, and even though I was 26 years old and a teacher, I suddenly realized that I knew nothing about sex at all. I mean, not at *all*.

"When I went back home that night, and got into bed with Douglas, I told him everything that we had talked about; and that I never had climaxes. He was quite shocked, not by the fact that I was talking about sex, he isn't a prude; but by the fact that I had never experienced a climax with him. So, in the end, I showed him how I masturbated; and he tried to copy how I did it. After about twenty minutes I suddenly found that I was very close to coming. After I had managed to climax once with Douglas, I found it very much easier the next time; and these days, four years later, even though I don't expect to have a climax every single time we make love, my body just doesn't seem to demand it, at least I'm satisfied."

Henrietta's preferred technique of masturbation

was to flick the very tip of her clitoris very lightly with her finger tips, very quickly. It didn't take her husband long to duplicate this technique, and add a few refinements of his own, such as inserting the fingers of his other hand into her vagina while he did so, and gently arousing that G-spot area just about three-quarters of an inch inside her vagina, toward the front.

"I don't know what my mother would think. I don't know what some of my friends would think. To tell you the truth, I don't care. Sometimes Douglas and I talk about the first five years of our marriage and how we nearly broke up because of the stresses and the arguments between us. And you wouldn't believe how often we kick ourselves that we let so many nights go by without having the kind of sex we're having now. It's made the difference between happiness and misery, believe me."

Now that we have talked about the clitoris, let's go a little further down and examine the urethra. This is the opening from which you urinate. Some women like to have their urethra mildly stimulated during sex, but many find it irritating. I have come across several incidents of women masturbating by inserting slender objects into their urinary opening, such as Q-Tips lubricated with soap or petroleum jelly, hairpins, even ball-point pens, but the dangers of infection or of losing the masturbatory object into your bladder make this kind of self-stimulation more risky than it's worth. I am all in favor of using any part of your body in any way that is both exciting and safe as part of your sexual repertoire; but pushing objects into your urethral opening is definitely not a good idea.

Ask your lover to try probing your urethral opening with the tip of his tongue; you may find that this is a fresh sensation that you enjoy. Of course, don't be worried if you don't.

Below your urethral opening is your vagina. As you start to explore it, you're going to realize just how absurd it is for anybody to think of it as a "hole."

In its usual relaxed state, your vagina is closed, with front and back walls meeting each other. If you gently insert your fingers into yourself, you will feel the lower, narrower part of the vagina—that part which those unromantic sex ressearchers call the "barrel"—but if you probe deeper you will reach into the wider part of the vagina called the "vault."

Actually, words such as "barrel" and "vault" are only coined by physiologists for the sake of accurate description, and I have yet to come across any of them who thinks of the female sexual organs as anything but exciting and entrancing.

When you first open your vagina to explore it, it should be light pink in color and moist on the inside. When you're sexually excited the moisture that your vagina exudes will be copious; and this (regardless of the embarrassment that many young girls feel when they find that their panties are wet after a first kiss) is not only normal and natural, but it is highly desirable. All of that moisture will help your lover's penis slide into you with the maximum of pleasure and the minimum of discomfort.

Until comparatively recently, it was thought that a woman's vaginal lubricating fluid came partly from the neck of her womb and partly from a pair of glands just inside her inner vaginal lips, called Bartholin's glands. But recent research with camera equipment actually placed inside women's vaginas during sexual excitement has shown that all of that "love juice" is exuded from the walls of the vaginal barrel itself, starting as droplets and then joining together to form a slippery and highly lubricative lining. This process appears to be caused by the swelling of the veins that form a network around the vaginal barrel, since the vagina itself has very few glands.

You don't have to explain all of this to your lover, but you should know what happens inside you when you make love. Knowledge gives confidence, and confident lovers are always better lovers.

Your vagina is formed out of an inner lining of mucous membrane that is soft and moist; and an outer lining that is muscular. The thin inner lining is folded into furrows, particularly at the back of your vagina and near its entrance. These furrows start to disappear in older women and in women who have had several children. By the time you reach the change of life, the menopause, you may find that they have disappeared altogether.

As you probe further up inside your vagina, into the "vault," you will be able to feel the neck of your womb protruding into it. At the front and at the back of the neck of the womb there are spaces that physiologists call the *fornices* of the vagina. It is into the rear *fornix*, just behind your cervix, that your lover's erect penis penetrates when you are making love.

Several fascinating changes take place inside your vagina as you become aroused for love. If you examine yourself as you masturbate, you will be able to see most of these changes taking place in front of your eyes.

As your vagina lubricates itself, it also begins to increase in length and to widen. Usually, the front and back walls of your vagina are in contact, but as you ready yourself for intercourse they separate and the furrows in the inner lining begin to flatten. The neck of the womb rises and moves forward in anticipation of accommodating your lover's penis, and the vault of your vagina opens wide. You will also notice as you become increasingly sexually excited that the color of the inside of your vagina grows darker, more purplish.

You can explore yourself several times to watch these changes occur. Then you can show them and explain them to your lover, so that he can share in the extraordinary magic of your vagina.

As you approach orgasm, the interior vault of your vagina opens wider, while the barrel grips your lover's penis even harder. Then, at the moment of orgasm, your vaginal muscles begin a series of anywhere from one to twenty spasms that start off intensely and then gradually diminish in frequency and strength.

After your climax, your vagina will gradually return to its "resting" size and state, while the neck of your womb will lower itself again so that it dips into the semen that your lover has ejaculated into you.

For your own enlightenment, it is worthwhile masturbating to orgasm in front of your mirror. You can watch what happens to your vagina as you become increasingly sexually aroused. You won't be able to see all of the changes that we've been discussing, but you'll certainly be able to see the swelling of your vaginal lips, the lubrication of the inner walls, and the change in color.

Once you have satisfied yourself that you are quite familiar with your vagina and your vulva, it's time to invite your lover to join you in your exploration so that he can see how you are made and how your body responds. His investigation of your vagina may very well lead to intense sexual arousal and intercourse; in fact it would be quite a happy ending to all of your exploration if it did.

Later on, we'll talk about how to explore *his* sexual organs, but just for now here's Jennifer, a 23-year-old air hostess from San Diego, who told me about this "sharing exploration" with her 29-year-old lover Paul.

"I'm lucky; I have a patio outside of my apartment that is secluded. When you told me to explore my own sexual organs someplace private, I knew that out on the patio was just the place. I guess you need someplace calm and restful and sunny to do something like that. And the truth about it was that I was actually quite frightened, even though that sounds silly. I think I'm sort of normal and well-balanced, but the idea of taking time out to examine yourself sexually—well, that's something quite new to me, although I understood the sense of it right from the very beginning.

"I took off all of my clothes and sat with my legs crossed and looked at my pussy in my make-up mirror. It was interesting just to look at it. You don't realize until you think about it what a kind of neat and attractive-looking part of your body your pussy is. I shave my pubic hair at the sides because I swim a lot, and wear very high-sided swimsuits, and I think I was quite pleased just at the way I looked. Anyway, I did everything you said and examined every part of myself. I was particularly interested in what you had to say about the clitoris. I started masturbating when I was only 11 or 12 years old, although I can feel myself blushing when I admit it. I used to have a silk scarf that my aunt had given me, and I started off by wearing it as a fancy-dress; but once, when I was playing Eastern princesses, I wore it as a kind of loincloth, and drew it between my legs. That gave me such a nice feeling that I kept on doing it; and when I was 14 I had my first climax, just by drawing the scarf up and down over my clitoris.

"I think I'm quite an intelligent, well-educated, well-adjusted kind of a person; but the truth is that I knew hardly anything about myself sexually; and that was why it was a tremendous revelation just to take a mirror and examine myself closely, guided by expert knowledge. It had never occurred to me to do it before, and in any case I think I would have been too reticent.

"About two weeks after, I mentioned to my boyfriend Carl what I had done, and I invited him to share the experience. At first he didn't know how to react. I guess he thought he knew all about women's bodies already, and didn't need any lessons, particularly from any kind of book. But when I told him that it was a little bit experimental, and that he might get mentioned in the book too, well, I think he was a little more enthusiastic after that.

"We sat out on my patio one Thursday afternoon in the sunshine, both of us naked. Carl had a hard-on even before we started; very hard; he has a magnificent cock, and it was all that I could do not to forget about the exploration and start fucking straight away. But I opened up my legs and showed him where my clitoris was, and how it was covered by its little hood, and what was the best way for him to rub it. Then I opened up wider and showed him my urethra, and my vagina, and explained to him, right from the book, reading it out to him, how my vagina changed when I was ready for sex. I let him slip his fingers right up inside me so that he could feel and understand everything. He was very turned-on, not just by the situation but by what he was learning, too. He wasn't embarrassed to learn; in fact, he said it made him feel more in control of what was going on; more confident. I could see that he was excited because his cock was shiny with lubricant, which I guess is the male equivalent to the fluid which a girl produces inside her vagina. But I told him he had to masturbate me first, to prove that he knew how to touch my clitoris. That's what he did; touching me very quickly and very lightly, silken fingers, that's what excites me; and it was tremendous. After only three of four minutes, I had to cling on to him because I had an orgasm, one of the most powerful orgasms I've ever experienced, and Carl was so excited by it that he had a climax, too, I've never seen a man climax like that before: he just suddenly shot out two or three bursts of come, all over my breasts.

"We lay there for a long time afterwards and discussed what had happened, and we both agreed that 'touching and exploring' had not only given us clear information, information that really helped us, it had also given us the excuse to get together and make love with lots of highly erotic foreplay. I know more about myself, Carl knows more about me, and both of us can't wait to read the rest of the book."

3

His Proudest Possession

When we discussed *your* sexual organs, I suggested that once you had familiarized yourself with how you were made and how you worked, you should let your lover or husband explore your body with you. Not only is such mutual exploration more enlightening than doing it on your own, it's more arousing.

Similarly, when finding out about your lover's sexual organs, you ought to ask him if you can investigate and manipulate them while actually reading through this chapter so that it won't be just an explanation on paper, which it inevitably has to be no matter how graphic I try to make it, but that it will be a living lesson in sexual anatomy and erotic response.

As you read, slowly stimulate your lover's sexual organs, until at the very end of the chapter you are able to make him ejaculate. That will complete the lesson and make him feel that it was all worth it. It will also be an interesting test of timing, not just for you, but for him. So this is the rule: No ejaculating until the very last word of the chapter, otherwise you'll have to go all the way back to the beginning and start again.

Sit side by side with your lover on the bed or on the sofa; make sure that the room is warm and that the atmosphere is quiet and comfortable. A little soft music never did any sexual encounter any harm, especially an exploration like this, which is going to be partly seductive and partly scientific.

Now take his penis in your hand. It may be soft, or the idea of having it caressed and investigated by you may already have hardened it. Its ability to rise up and down is an indication of its dual function—to act as a tube to carry urine out of your lover's bladder, at which time it is very much more convenient and comfortable for it to be flaccid, and to shoot semen deep inside your vagina, when obviously it has to be hard and erect and pointing upward. Although the textbooks never talk about it, I always say that the penis has a third function, which has nothing whatsoever to do with the passing of urine or semen; and that is simply to please a woman by stimulating the inside of her vagina or mouth or anus. Sexual intercourse is important not just for reproduction but for achieving that emotional closeness without which we would all find it very much harder to live and work and talk together as emotionally balanced human beings.

Inside the penis there are three spongy columns of tissue that give it the ability to rise and fall. Squeeze it and feel them. At the top and sides are two corpora cavernosa, which at their lower end are attached to the pelvic bones. Beneath these bodies of tissue lies the corpus spongiosum, which also makes up the head or "knob" of the penis.

As soon as your lover becomes sexually excited, blood vessels inside all of these three columns of tissue open up, and blood quickly fills them up, stiffening his penis and enlarging it. The blood vessels leading *away* from his penis, however, are almost completely closed off so his penis remains erect, like a balloon filled with water that can't escape.

In men who are not circumcised, the hardening of their penises will lead to their foreskins rolling back, revealing the naked head or *glans* as it is usually called. The glans is reddish-purple and, as you can see, divided just below the tip to provide an exit both for urine and semen. You may delicately touch and fondle the opening with your fingers; the sensation to your lover is very slightly irritating but highly arousing. If you give the shaft of his penis three or four vigorous strokes with your hand, you may very well see in that opening the first signs of clear, slippery sexual lubricant, which is often produced by a man during the early stages of erotic excitement.

As far as circumcision is concerned, sex researchers William Masters and Virginia Johnson came up with proof that it has no effect whatsoever one way or another on sexual performance. The belief used to be that circumcised men could satisfy their women better: The reason for this being that the constant friction of clothing against their exposed glans gradually dulled their sexual sensitivity and therefore allowed them to make love to their women much longer before reaching their own climax. Comprehensive laboratory tests indicated that uncircumcised men reach a climax no faster or slower than circumcised men.

The glans of your lover's penis, just like your clitoris, is thick with sensitive nerve receptors. It is the friction of your vagina against these nerves that will eventually bring your man to a climax.

Now (keeping up that slow systematic stimulation of your lover's penis) turn your attention to the wrinkled bag of skin beneath his penis—his *scrotum*. Inside, the scrotum is divided into two separate compartments, and each compartment contains a *testis*. Practically every man in the world has his left testis hanging marginally lower than his right. Even Michaelangelo's famous sculpture of David has his left testis hanging lower than his right. But the testes are both attached to a system of muscles that can raise them up and down, either in response to the threat of being hurt or struck or in response to changes in temperature. When a man's body is cold, his testes rise up toward his body cavity; when he is warm, they sink lower.

This rising and falling is done to keep the testes at about 95 degrees Fahrenheit, which is slightly lower than the temperature inside the body itself. High temperatures discourage the efficient production of sperm; and although I have never taken the information particularly seriously, some sex researchers claim that if a man wears tight-fitting trousers or briefs or spends too much time bicycle riding, his sperm production can be seriously affected by the extra heat generated between his legs.

Each testis contains about 250 compartments, and each compartment contains several tightly rolled-up tubes over two feet long, called *seminiferous tubules*. It is in these tubes that the sperms are first developed, and there are billions of them produced every day. All the tubes join together on the top of the testis to form another coiled-up tube that is nearly 20 feet long, called the *epididymis*, which means, literally, outside the twin—the twins being the testes. It is into the epididymis that the sperms flow as they are produced, and it is here that they wait until they are called for by muscular spasm or until they die (after about a fortnight) from neglect.

The epididymis leads into another tube called the *vas deferens*, which is about a foot and a half long and takes a scenic route around the pubic bone, down behind the bladder, and into the base of the penis.

There are two vas deferens—two vasa deferentia, if we have to be grammatical about it—one from each testis. On their way around the scenic route, each of them is joined by a duct from those two small glands called seminal vesicles, which produce the first part of your lover's semen.

Then they pass through his prostate gland, and there they collect chemicals that stimulate contractions in your womb after you've made love—and are probably designed to help his sperm make their way up inside your uterus.

Inside the prostate gland, the two vasa deferentia join together and enter the urethra, which is the tube that connects the bladder to the penis. Just beyond the prostate they are joined by yet more glands, all of which contribute fluid to lubricate the head of his penis when he has sex with you and to sustain his sperm with oxygen and sugars so that they can survive and swim once they have been ejaculated.

You can see now that inside those comparatively simple-looking organs a great many complicated and technical things are going on to produce not only sexual satisfaction but efficient reproduction—not that you may be as interested in the second as you are in the first. But it's all part of the process and all bound up in the psychology and physiology of erotic delight.

Sexually, men have traditionally been faced with a burdensome role. They have been expected throughout the centuries to be the sexual aggressor, the one who "conquers" the woman. As we have seen from the previous chapter in which we discussed the value of coming on strong when you find a man who takes your fancy, however, men are just as much in need of sexual reassurance as women. If you're clever about it, though, you can make sure that he *feels* as if he's "conquering" you, which will do a great deal for his confidence in bed and to *your* sexual pleasure. You can make sure that he has quicker, longer-lasting, and harder erections; and for you that can only be good news, particularly if you're the kind of woman who's a l-i-t-t-l-e slower in reaching a climax.

(Are you still massaging his penis? Keep at it.)

The most onerous part of sex for a man is getting and keeping an erection. Whereas a woman is always ready for sexual intercourse, a man is incapable of penetration unless he has a reasonable hard-on. An added problem is that he has no conscious control whatsoever over the rise and fall of his penis. He can think all the dirty thoughts in the world, but if his penis won't come up, then it won't come up. This condition, when it happens regularly, is called *primary impotence*. In 90 percent of cases, primary impotence is *functional* rather than *organic*—that is to say that it is caused by worry or tiredness or fear rather than by anything medically wrong.

Most cases of funcitonal impotence can be cleared up if you and your lover face up to whatever difficulties may be causing it and discuss them freely. Sometimes, functional impotence can be caused by something as simple as the fact that your lover is working hard at the office and when he comes back he needs sleep rather than sex. If he can't manage to have sex with you, he feels guilty and unmanly, and that introduces a new element of stress that is likely to make his impotence even worse.

There are incidents when functional impotence is deep rooted in a childhood sexual trauma. (One man saw his mother having sex with his father, her legs wide apart, and every time his young wife opened up her thighs for him he suddenly found his erection dying away.) Sometimes, as I have mentioned, it is caused by stress at work. At other times, it may be connected to other romantic problems, particularly during middle age.

A 40-year-old friend of mine became desperately infatuated with his young secretary at the office, but he found to his shame and chagrin that he was incapable of sex either with her or with his wife. In the end, he had to give in gracefully, admit that the strain of an extramarital affair would be too much for him on top of a key executive post, and tell his secretary thanks, but no thanks.

So many sexual problems can be solved when you have understanding partners and when you can freely discuss your worries and your upsets out in the open. Impotence, more than any other sexual difficulty, seems to respond to frank discussion.

This means that you, as the woman in your man's life, have a special responsibility if the problem of impotence ever arises. It's up to you to be understanding; it's up to you to make sure that he doesn't feel unmanly and useless; it's up to you to coax back that erection without which a satisfactory sexual relationship simply doesn't exist.

"When Ronnie was appointed manager at work, our sex life went completely out of the window," said 33-year-old Charlene, from Milwaukee, Wisconsin. "He came home bushed every evening and never wanted to make love; and on those occasions when I did manage to tease him and tickle him, he lost his erection almost straight away. I was beginning to snap at him because I was feeling frustrated; but the trouble is, that made him feel even worse and even less adequate, and in the end we both seriously began to think about leaving each other. I mean, the tension was terrific, you could have cut it with a pair of scissors.

"I began to have sexual fantasies when I was in bed at night, and masturbate during the day. The trouble was, by the fantasizing and masturbating I was creating my own sexual satisfaction away from my relationship from Ronnie, and he began to sense that I was drifting away from him, that I no longer really cared whether he got an erection or not, and that must have been just about the killer. So I sat down and thought about it, and then I had a talk with Ronnie. I mean we just talked about his penis not coming up. At first he was aggressive, and I was aggressive back, but in the end I asked him to come upstairs and give me an orgasm, no matter how he did it, whether he used his penis or his tongue or whatever. We lay on the bed. I remember it clearly because it was a sunny Thursday afternoon, and you could hear people walking along the sidewalk outside.

"He kissed me, and kissed my breasts, and sucked my nipples, and kind of drummed them on the roof of his mouth with his tongue. I always liked that. Then he started to caress my thighs and my stomach, and then open up my pussy. He licked me first of all, very *very* gently with the absolute tip of his tongue, and that began to start up a feeling in me after a while that made me shift my hips and moan and start to move, but he kept on licking me and licking me, and I could feel my juices flowing; they flowed right down between the cheeks of my bottom and that's when he wet his finger in them and worked it slowly into my ass, very deep, and it was at that moment even before I expected it that an orgasm started, kind of slow at first and then suddenly so fierce that I couldn't control it. Then he made love to me. He was hard, he was hard again, and he made love to me. It was so beautiful I had tears in my eyes."

Charlene's sexual problems with Ronnie weren't solved overnight; there were many more incidents of functional impotence before their lovemaking began to return to its previous level of satisfaction. But once they had *both* faced up to what was wrong, and Charlene had helped Ronnie to take positive steps to overcome it, without recrimination, without blame, and most of all without making him feel that she thought he didn't love her anymore—then the incidents occurred less and less frequently. One week, they both suddenly realized that their lovemaking was completely back to normal.

Premature ejaculation—when a man climaxes far too quickly, leaving his sex partner unsatisfied—is a form of impotence in itself.

Case histories of the kind of man who suffers from premature ejaculation show that he is likely to be an isolated, private sort of a person, who expresses his feelings either by shutting himself away or by aggressive overassertion. You can see why so many of those men who behave like Obnoxious Bastards with women tend to be unable to satisfy women even when they have succeeded in attracting them. In fact, their obnoxiousness often hides the fact that they feel unsure of themselves, uncertain of their standing with women; and when they come to the point of making love, a combination of stress and overexcitement leads them to shoot their load almost straight away. There is a considerable gap in any event between the time it takes for a man to become aroused and for a woman to become aroused. When a man suffers from premature ejaculation, the gap becomes frustratingly wider.

Nobody can tell how many women lie unsatisfied in bed at night, while their lovers or husbands lie snoring obliviously beside them, little realizing that they have completely failed to give them any kind of sexual joy. If you are one of those women, then the time has come for you not only to speak out but to do something practical about it. It will be for *his* benefit, as well as yours.

For years, couples tried to solve the problem of premature ejaculation by using the "no-touch" method; that is, the woman did not touch or stroke her lover's genitals in any way before penetration. The trouble with no touch was that it was no good. As soon as the man inserted his penis into his wife or lover, the instant excitement was more than enough to make him ejaculate.

Probably the best practical method of dealing with premature ejaculation so far devised is that explained by Drs. Masters and Johnson in their research for *Human Sexual Inadequacy*. I want you to try this method now with your husband or lover if you have him there with you so that you can see for yourself that it works.

Rub your lover's penis until it is erect. If he has an impulse to ejaculate, place your thumb on the underside of the penis on that little bridge of skin called the frenulum, just below the opening, and your first and second fingers on either side of the ridge on the top of the penis; then squeeze until he loses his urge to ejaculate. Stimulate him again. Then, as he approaches his climax, squeeze again. You will find that you can hold back his climax for up to half an hour—or until you're ready to have him slip inside you and shoot his semen.

It almost always works—and it's a very positive first step in helping him to satisfy both himself and you. The next stage is for you to try intercourse—making sure every time that your lover warns you when he is about to climax so that you can take out his penis and squeeze it so that he doesn't ejaculate until you *both* want him to.

One of the added benefits about this technique as far as *you're* concerned is that it concentrates your mind on your own sexual pleasure, as well as his, and that you will be very strongly motivated toward your own orgasmic release.

Masters and Johnson reported a very high success rate with this "squeeze method"; there isn't any doubt at all that their practical experience with sexual therapy brought about some revolutionary changes in the way that men and women were prepared to think about helping themselves and each other.

That is the great value of being an independent, liberated woman when it comes to matters of sex. At last you can openly say what you want, and what you expect, and take a practical part in getting it. You expect orgasms? Then you shall have them. You expect a man who satisfies you completely? You can actively assist him to become a more effective and more exciting lover. Similarly, you should expect your lover to help you with any problems that you might have, such as difficulty in reaching orgasm or an aversion to oral sex or to any other variety of sex that *he* would like to try and that *you* don't relish. More of that later, however.

Now that you have an idea of how your lover's sex organs are put together, let's see what happens as you bring him toward a climax.

As he enters what sexologists call the *plateau phase* of excitement—that pleasurable buildup that immediately precedes his climax—his penis will secrete a small amount of slippery, lubricating fluid. What you ought to know about this fluid is that it often contains living sperms, and so it is quite possible for you to become pregnant even before your lover has reached his climax. So much for the famed withdrawal method of contraception.

As I have said, this fluid does have a lubricating effect, but modern researchers now believe that lubrication is not its primary function. In fact, they don't quite know *what* it's for, although when it appears it's usually a sign that your lover is controlling his climax to suit your level of excitement, since it isn't secreted so frequently during masturbation or oral sex when he will usually be trying to reach a climax as quickly as possible.

As your man's climax approaches, he will start to breathe heavily and then to pant. His heart rate will go up from a normal 72 beats per minute to 110 or even 175 beats per minute. He will start to thrust more rapidly into you and clutch at you in order to increase the depth of his penetration. Then comes a moment when he can no longer delay his climax—the moment of *ejaculatory inevitability* to give it its Sunday name—and in the space of from two to five seconds before actual climax the following takes place:

- The prostate gland contracts rhythmically, squeezing out the fluid that forms the basis of male semen. The seminal vesicles add their fluid, too. As they discharge, the sperms stored in the vas deferens are ejected into the urethra to complete the mix.
- The internal muscle that controls the bladder contracts, simultaneously sealing the bladder so that no semen is forced into it and sealing the urethra behind the semen so that it only has one way to go, and that's out through the penis and into you.
- Then the external muscle controlling the bladder relaxes, in direct contrast to every other muscle in the male pelvis, allowing the semen to flood into a wider part of the urethra, which is exactly like the bulb of an eyedropper. As soon as this bulb is filled with sufficient semen, it contracts sharply and the semen is ejaculated out through the penis.

At the same time, two large muscles in the floor of the pelvis start to spasm, adding to the force of the ejaculation. If your vagina didn't happen to be in the way, the semen could be shot anything up to two or three feet across the room. As a matter of academic interest, semen travels at an average of 28 miles per hour.

There are usually three or four spasms, occurring every second or so. Then they die away, and very quickly the penis begins to relax.

As far as comparative sensations of pleasure are concerned, men tend to experience their greatest enjoyment in that very first spurt of semen, particularly after a long period of sexual abstinence. Even the second and third spurts of the same climax are not quite as delightful as the first. Women, on the other hand, often prefer the later spasms of their orgasms to the first; and when they experience two or three orgasms in one sexual encounter, they express a distinct preference for the later orgasms over the earlier ones.

Men are not capable of multiple orgasms. Once they have climaxed, their sexual organs have to go through what is called a *refractory period*, which may last from fifteen minutes to several hours. During this refractory period, all of those stimulations that excited him so much during the buildup to his climax—especially rubbing and sucking his penis— will not only do nothing very much for him, they may positively irritate him.

If you haven't achieved your orgasm by the time your lover ejaculates, then his sudden disinterest in sexual arousal is obviously going to be acutely disappointing and frustrating for you. Unfortunately, you have to live with the physiological and psychological fact that as soon as he has climaxed, the intensity of your partner's erotic interest in you will abruptly dissipate.

That is why it is crucially important for you to make it clear to him that you have not yet climaxed and to urge him to see his ejaculation not as the completion of the act of making love, but simply as a part of it. No act of making love can be considered to have ended until *both* partners are satisfied and relaxed and have shared between them all the pleasure they need and deserve.

Now it may be that once he has ejaculated, you do not wish to be stimulated right up to orgasm straight away; you may prefer to wait until he is capable of stirring up another erection. But when that happens, you will have to make quite sure that your orgasm is the first priority. It may be twenty minutes later, it may be the following morning, but it's still part of the same act of love, and now it's *your* turn to be pleasured.

Believe me, that philosophy isn't as me-oriented as it sounds. He will derive just as much satisfaction from satisfying you as you do.

If he has ejaculated just before you were about to reach orgasm and you are highly stimulated and want to continue, then you can coax him into doing his duty in several ways. You can either tell him, "go on," and leave it to him to think of a method of bringing you up to your climax; or you can take his hand and press it against your vulva so that he realizes you want him to masturbate you to orgasm; or you can exhort him to go down on you and give you a climax orally.

Many men find the experience of licking a woman into whose vagina they have just ejaculated quite arousing, and you may find that by the time you are reaching your climax, he is rearing up again and ready for more, in which case you may be in line for a series of multiple orgasms.

Another unexpected benefit was discovered by 19-year-old Marguerite, a music student from New York. "Even though I had been living with Simon for nearly a year, I had never been very enthusiastic about giving him head, mainly because I couldn't stand the thought of having to taste his come. But one evening after we'd finished a bottle of wine we went to bed; and after he'd climaxed, he went down on me and brought me off by kissing me and licking me. Then he came up and kissed me on my mouth, and of course his mouth and cheeks were all covered in his own come. I suddenly realized that the taste wasn't at all what I had imagined it to be. It's kind of bitter in a funny sort of way, it can make your mouth feel dry; but ever since then I've never had any aversion to swallowing it or licking it."

As you gradually stimulate your lover toward the end of this chapter, it's worth saying a word or two about the *size* of his penis. Men's penises do vary in size, but generally the difference is only a matter of millimeters; and there is less variation between erect penises than there is between soft penises. So a penis that may look small when it's unstimulated may grow to very respectable proportions when it's aroused.

There is such muscular elasticity in your vagina that the size of your lover's penis will make no difference at all to your lovemaking. The only difficulty you may ever encounter if your lover is especially well-endowed is in anal intercourse, and then a lubricant like K-Y jelly is usually sufficient to overcome any reluctance by your muscles to accommodate him.

Some men vainly try to enlarge the size of their penises, either by masturbating furiously or by using creams or so-called penile developers. The creams, of course, are completely useless. One is advertised as "Spanish Fly Hard-On Erection Cream" and is said to "increase the swelling capacity of the male sexual organ." Three jars sell for $20. The penile developers are perspex tubes (transparent cylinders sealed at one end by a vacuum valve), into which the developee inserts his penis and from which he extracts all the air by means of a rudimentary pump. Since nature abhors a vacuum, his penis will expand to fill the interior of the vacated tube. These tubes are made of acrylic so that their owners can look down and admire their newly enlarged penises with pride. Unfortunately, as soon as the vacuum is released and the penis is removed from the perspex tube, the penis returns to its normal size.

There is absolutely no way in which a man can physically increase the size of his penis, so if your lover is ever tempted to try a cream or a developer, tell him to save his money. Developers aren't cheap —anything upwards of $50—and their sales pitch is insidious.

"The man who possesses a fully enlarged, fully-trained, peak-performance penis [Makes it sound like a pedigree dog, doesn't it?] need not worry how a woman will compare him with other men. He will know well enough from the actions of her body and the look on her face. [And the way she says, 'Do you have a fully enlarged, fully-trained, peak performance penis'?] He will have more confidence in every way because he will be MORE OF A MAN."

This is the text from an advertisement that includes the Piston Action Stroker, which is said to have produced "many recorded penis growths of up to four and one-half inches." Price: $36.

What makes any man's penis effective is not its size or even the way it's trained. It's the care and affection and skill with which a man makes love that counts.

Of course, if your lover mistakenly believes that his penis is smaller than it ought to be, it will be very difficult to persuade him otherwise. All you can do is give it the very best attention you can, and he will soon realize that you love it not for its size, but for what pleasure it can give you.

Now, you can bring him to that well-deserved climax, in any way you like.

4

The Shape of Sex

When I wrote *How to Drive Your Man Wild in Bed* ten years ago, I introduced the then-revolutionary notion of physical exercise exclusively to help you improve your sex life. Since then, of course, physical fitness has become an internationally accepted ideal, and men and women all over the world are reaping the erotic benefits of keeping in shape. But even if you've been jogging and swimming and keeping up those aerobic classes, there are still extra exercises that you can do specifically to improve your talents in bed.

It is very important to keep your thighs, your back, and your pelvic muscles in reasonable trim, because it is the muscles in these parts of your body that will help you the most when you are making love. This is true except for the muscles that surround your vagina, and later on in this chapter I will be giving you some intimate exercises that will help you to develop an astonishing vaginal grip and flexibility.

Fitness not only gives you the ability to make love better and longer, it improves your confidence and your self-image and generally makes you look better and feel more sexually attractive. That is not to say that you have to slim and train until you're as thin as a strand of spaghetti in order to attract the man you want. Most men are rather put off by women who are too fit and too skinny and too physically competitive; some men even have a very distinct preference for girls who are Abundant with a capital A. *Playboy* in March, 1984, ran a pictorial of big voluptuous girls and drew a notably enthusiastic response. Said one reader, "I wanted to bury my face in your pages and wallow in unabashed gluttony."

Men have as varied a sexual taste in women as women have in men. I know at least two men who cannot stand the sight of Bo Derek. I know at least 200 men who would pay money not to be locked in a bedroom with Joan Collins. One friend of mine fell in love with Jayne Mansfield from a picture in a magazine and was just about ready to throw himself off the Coronado Bay Bridge when he realized that she was no longer available for anything but spiritual relationships. Another friend of mine deliberately avoids looking at pictures of Dolly Parton, simply because he knows he will never be able to fondle that Valkyrie-like bosom. In the days when I was working for *Penthouse* magazine there would be fierce arguments among the staff about voluptuous girls ("too fat!") or trim girls ("looks like a skeleton!")

My feeling is that provided you keep yourself reasonably fit, you should avoid strenuous diets and relentless exercise, especially if your motive for jogging and weight lifting and starving yourself of everything but grapefruit-flavored yogurt and gooseberry salad is to make yourself more attractive to men. You will *always* be more attractive, especially in bed, if you are relaxed and happy with yourself and not overobsessed with the way you look.

Never apologize to any man for the appearance of your naked body, your breasts, your stomach, your thighs, or anything. He took you to bed because he found you attractive as you are; you don't have to point out faults that, even if they really *are* faults, he can see for himself. By doing that, you're not only going to make him feel that he has to compliment you ("Don't be silly I think your breasts are *beautiful*"), you're indirectly criticizing his taste in women. Now—had you ever thought about that? So whatever you feel like saying, don't say it. Enjoy his compliments; enjoy the fact that you turn him on; and if you're really worried about your stomach and your thighs, make a firm resolve that you're going to work on them a little more and not eat any more cream-filled pastries every time you're feeling a nibble of hunger at work.

The shape of good sex is the shape you are and the shape you want to be. Whether you burst out of a 38DD or you scarcely fill a 34A, there are ways of dressing and of acting that can make the most of whatever you have—or haven't—got. We'll talk about dressing erotically later; but the main thing is to remember that, provided you're reasonably fit, it doesn't matter *what* shape you are. Whatever impression you may get from the movies or TV commercials, every single woman is a different shape from every other woman, and to kill yourself trying to look like Christie Brinkley (unless that's your natural physique) is not only time wasting but could be physically and psychologically damaging.

"My boyfriend Lannie said he only liked really thin girls. I think I was quite skinny at the time, but I started to starve myself so that I would match up to Lannie's ideal of what a beautiful woman should look like. He would point out women in the street, on advertisements, or on television. 'Look at that,' he'd say, 'you could circle her waist with your two hands.' For some reason, that really turned him on. So I ate hardly anything for two months, and went to aerobic classes for two hours every night, and believe me that kind of skinny look wasn't me at all. I looked awful, like they'd just let me out of Belsen or something, and I knew that I'd never look any better. I kept fainting at work, and when it came to making love, I didn't have the energy or the inclination to be interested, apart from the fact that I was always hungry. In the end, I collapsed when I was getting off the crosstown bus, and I was taken to the hospital. I talked to a doctor and then I talked to a psychiatrist. The psychiatrist said I was right on the brink of anorexia nervosa, and that if I tried to go on starving myself and exercising so hard, I'd die. Too much strain on the heart, you know what I mean? So I said to the psychiatrist, 'What am I going to say to my boyfriend?' and he said, 'Tell him to shove it up his ass.' I was so shocked that I said, 'Are you really a qualified doctor?'"

That was Stefanie, a 26-year-old publishing assistant from New York City. Stefanie has the kind of figure that Jewish people rather pleasantly call *zaftig*. She looks beautiful that way; and what's more, she is very fit. She plays squash once a week, she swims twice a week, and she goes jogging in the park with her dog Pluto on weekends. She has given up the boyfirend who insisted on seeing her ribs and instead has been having a "happy and very hot" affair with a senior executive at the publishing company where she works.

Now she says, "I'm happy with myself, the way I look. I'll always have big breasts and heavy thighs and a big bottom and a rounded stomach. That's me, that's the way I'm made. If ever I start to feel that I'm really *too* plump, I remind myself that I can run two miles without panting, and then I go look at the poster I've pinned up in my bathroom, a painting by Rubens called *The Toilet of Venus*. That painting is guaranteed to make any woman feel thin by comparison; and yet here was a woman whom Rubens thought was gorgeously beautiful, and so she is."

You can get yourself into reasonably good shape simply by following an exercise-oriented routine when you're at home or at work. Here's my basic regime for improving your day-to-day (and night-to-night) condition just by being a little less lazy around the office or around the house. If you keep to this regime for two or three months, and believe me it isn't difficult, you'll begin to find that you're very much sounder in wind and limb and that when it comes to lovemaking you have far more stamina and far more capacity, not only for enjoying your orgasms but for having them earlier.

Being able to reach a climax sooner is an important factor in improving your love life and satisfying your lover and yourself. The biological fact is that women are sexually aroused much more slowly than men (we've already seen how much longer it takes the clitoris to reach a condition of sexual tumescence than the penis) and, consequently, the most common sexual problem is that of the man ejaculating before the woman is ready to climax and leaving her unsatisfied time after time. You know the problem. Almost every woman has experienced it at one time or another.

If you're more fit, however, you should be able to participate more actively in intercourse and use your pelvic and vaginal muscles to increase your own stimulation, as well as that of your lover. And if that leads to your climaxing sooner—at the same time as your lover or even *before*—then the benefits are obvious. You will be having more climaxes, and

he will be experiencing all the pride and the pleasure of knowing that he has satisfied you properly.

Here are some general tips on keeping yourself
alert and active during the day. Then, we'll get into
some formal exercises.

- When you're in the office, make a point of getting up and visiting anybody you need to talk to
  rather than telephoning. In fact, every half
  hour or so, get up from your desk and do something, even if it's nothing more productive than
  looking out of the window for a while. Don't sit
  in one position for long periods of time.

- Exercise your eyes as well as your body. If you
  have to type a lot or read a lot, lift your eyes
  away from your typewriter or your reading ma-
  terial every now and again and refocus them
  into the distance.

- Sometimes work can induce a high degree of
  stress. If you feel yourself reaching the boiling
  point, force yourself to stop whatever it is that
  you're doing, sit back in your chair for a while,
  and then gradually shake yourself loose. Breathe
  in and out slowly and calmly.

- If you're at home, try to make a point of walking somewhere out of the house at least once a
  day, even if it's just around the yard. When you
  go shopping, make that little extra effort not to
  park right outside the store. A short walk
  across the parking lot will do you an immeasur-
  able amount of good. And if you're feeling lone-
  some or depressed, *don't* go to the food cup-
  board, *don't* take an alcoholic drink, *don't* flop
  down and watch television. Instead, get yourself out of the house and walk or jog, and start
  thinking how lucky you are that you're alive
  and active.

- At work, take the stairs rather than the elevator. Stair climbing is one of the most rigorous exercises and is particularly good for the thighs and the shins.

- Whenever you can, kick off your shoes and roll your ankles around. Point your toes like a ballerina, then flex the ankles back again. Take off socks or pantyhose and wriggle your toes around.
- If you have to type a great deal, stop once in a while and clench your fists; then throw out your fingers in quick, rapid movements, stretching them as far as you can.
- Above all, make a point of promising yourself as you go through every day that you're going to keep as physically active as you are mentally active. Exaggerate every gesture you make; do everything with zest and a deliberate flourish. Not only will it help you to keep fitter and more alert, it will make you a better and brighter person for everybody to know.

Here are four exercises that you should do at least twice a day, especially when you're at work. They are additional and complementary to any aerobic dancing or fitness program that you may be doing at the moment, and they have been prepared in cooperation with a Chinese lady who is qualified in tai chi, which is an exercise and martial arts discipline specifically concerned with balancing the feminine and masculine elements in nature and of making the very best use of your internal life force (your chi).

On their own, these exercises will keep you in moderately good shape, provided you remember to do them regularly. If you do them in addition to any other fitness program you may be going through, you will find that they will enhance whatever benefits you are already enjoying, without disturbing or unbalancing the regime that your present teacher has given you.

They are all designed to be done in a chair, so that you can run through them at work without difficulty or inconvenience; if somebody happens to come into your office unexpectedly, you can always pretend that you were looking for a dropped pencil.

First, sit upright in your chair, with your back as straight as you can make it. Clasp your hands behind your back, palms upward, so that the backs of your wrists are resting just above your bottom. Now, flex your shoulder blades as close together as you can, and at the same time see how close together your elbows can get. Do this ten times, breathing evenly and as deeply as you do so.

Second, sit upright in your chair, with your back straight. Place your feet flat on the floor. Then cross your hands over your chest, quite lightly, keeping your elbows tucked in to the side of your body. Breathing easily and normally, turn your head as far as you can to the right, and hold it there for a count of ten. Then turn to the left, and repeat.

Third, sit with your back straight, your feet flat on the floor, and your stomach pulled in. Then clasp your right leg just below the knee and raise your leg up to your chest. See if you can touch your forehead with your knee. Repeat this exercise with each leg five times.

Fourth, sit up very straight in your chair, and rest your hands on your hips. Lift your right leg until it is level with your hip, keeping your foot upright, and then flex your thigh muscle five times. Repeat the exercise five times with each leg.

As simple as these exercises sound, they have been very carefully worked out to give you the maximum fitness from the minimum amount of daily effort.

While you are continuing these all-over exercises,

you will need to start concentrating on exercises that develop your vaginal muscles. The simplest exercise of all, of course, is to tighten and release your vaginal muscles as often as you can while sitting at your desk or even watching TV, having dinner, or waiting at a traffic signal in your car. Work on your anal muscles, too, and the muscles that contract your entire lower pelvic area. It is extraordinary how complicated an exercise regime you can go through without anybody noticing, just while you're sitting down; and it will all help you to be a far more active lover.

For several important reasons in your development to be the kind of woman who can really drive her man wild in bed, you should try to masturbate every single day, even if you can't manage to reach a climax on every single occasion. If it becomes a part of your daily sexual routine, you will grow far less inhibited about masturbation, and you will see it for what it is—a way of stimulating yourself, exercising yourself, and learning about yourself. Also, as we saw from the touching and exploring we did in the previous chapter, masturbation when done with your lover can be part of a very rewarding sexual encounter.

It may not always be possible, but do try to set aside ten or fifteen minutes or even longer during your day for intimate exercises. During that time, shower and massage yourself with lightly perfumed oil, paying particular attention to those parts that arouse you the most—your breasts, thighs, bottom, and, ultimately, your vulva. Be as slow and sensual as you want to be; after all, this is your body and it's really worth caring for. Play some of your favorite music if you want to; try to relax away the stresses and strains of the day and think of all the warm erotic things you'd like to be doing instead of working or cleaning the house.

Start by massaging the outer lips of your vagina; then stimulate your clitoris in the way that you find the most exciting. As the juice begins to flow in your vagina, insert one finger, as far as you can, and squeeze your muscles rhythmically. Then insert two fingers, and squeeze again, twenty or thirty times.

You may already own a vibrator. If you do, it can be an invaluable aid in vaginal exercises. Insert it into your vagina, and try to draw it into you by the power of your muscles alone; then see if you can expel it. You should try this exercise twenty times every day, because the control it will give you over your vaginal "barrel" will be remarkable. After a few weeks, you should be able to slide the vibrator in and out of you, using your vaginal muscles alone, with speed and ease.

If you don't own a vibrator, then I recommend that you buy one—not as a penis substitute, but as an instrument in its own right for helping you improve your sexual technique and increase your erotic pleasure. Remember that your vagina is a beautiful organ in itself, and if it can best be stimulated and exercised by the insertion of fingers, a hairbrush handle, or a vibrator, then it should be, and you certainly should have nothing to feel ashamed about. If you're at all embarrassed about going into a sex-aid ship or a drugstore to buy a vibrator, then try the classified advertisements in almost any girlie magazine like *Chic* or *Hustler*; but usually you'll find that your friendly neighborhood druggist will serve you what you want without raising an eyebrow.

In many ways, a solid latex dildo is preferable to a vibrator, and for that you will definitely have to go to your local sex store. The advantage of a latex dildo is that it is far more pliable than a vibrator, which has a hard plastic casing and remains rigid even when you cover it with a penis-shaped latex sleeve. With a dildo, you can flex your vaginal muscles more freely, and if you feel daring enough, you can follow Karen's example. Karen is a 21-year-old dance teacher from La Jolla, California.

"I bought a dildo once when I was living on my own for three months without a boyfriend. I used to find that there were times when I got almost uncontrollably horny, and the only way in which I could satisfy myself was to take the dildo to bed with me and masturbate with it, sometimes for an hour at a time. I learned to do all kinds of things with that dildo; I learned that I could have six or seven orgasms one after the other. I also learned how to delay my orgasm by relaxing my muscles and how to make it happen more quickly by tightening them. I realized gradually that it was helping me to develop my internal muscles, and since I knew quite a lot about dance and how dancing developed my external muscles, I began to understand that I was really doing myself some good.

"Occasionally I used to insert the dildo into my pussy, with a pair of tight swimsuit pants to make sure that it stayed inside me, and I would take a walk down to the beach or go window shopping along Prospect Street, squeezing it and flexing it inside me as I walked. It gave me some fantastic sensations, particularly when I thought that all those people walking around me had no idea that I had a dildo right up inside me. Sometimes I would get back to my apartment in such a high state of sexual arousal that I would close the door behind me and thrust my hand into my panties and masturbate right then and there, in the hall, just to relieve the feelings that had built up inside me.

"I have a steady boyfriend now, and all of those pent-up sexual frustrations tend to get dealt with very happily. But he's very appreciative of all of my muscular control; and, believe me, so am I; and if I hadn't used my dildo, I don't think I ever could have developed it to such a fantastic pitch.''

Karen's use of a dildo was provocative and sophisticated, although the practice of walking around with a simulated penis inserted in the vagina must be sufficiently widespread for at least two manufacturers of sexual aids to produce latex panties with a built-in dildo, and one pair with *two* dildos of different sizes for simultaneous vaginal and anal insertion.

We are getting into the realm of more advanced and unusual sexual practices. Don't feel that you have to wear a dildo inside you all day in order to become the kind of woman who can satisfy your man more than any other woman he's ever met. But do consider buying either a vibrator or a dildo in order to train your vaginal muscles to the highest possible level of erotic versatility. Karen is actually capable of making a pencil slide in and out of her vagina simply by using her internal muscles.

Many women have asked me about masturbation—whether it's harmful, whether it can somehow interfere with their sexual relationships with their husbands or lovers, whether it amounts to a betrayal of the man they love.

I can understand their fears and their reservations, because such a fierce campaign against masturbation was waged in Victorian times, particularly by fanatics like Henry Varley, who publicly denounced the "terrible and destructive sin of Onanism or self-abuse—a practice as common as it is hateful and injurious." It was decades before most men and women stopped feeling guilty about masturbating; and, unfortunately, many still do. This is despite the fact that Dr. Alfred Kinsey's epoch-making sexual studies in 1953 and 1948 showed that at some time of their lives, almost all

men and well over half of all women have masturbated regularly.

So to reassure those anxious women who ask me
about masturbation, all I can say is that it is not
harmful in any way at all, that it cannot interfere in
any way with your lovemaking, and that it cannot
be construed by any stretch of the imagination as
"betraying" your partner, even if you fantasize
about a different man when you do it. After all, a
great many women fantasize about different men,
even when they're actually having intercourse with
the men they're making love with.

Regard masturbation as a relief, a pleasure, and
an exercise. As one woman said to me recently, "If
God hadn't wanted me to masturbate, he would
have made my arms too short to reach between my
legs."

Meanwhile, don't forget those all-over exercises
and genital-stimulation exercises. One set comple-
ments the other; and between them you can shape
up for the kind of sex that *you* need and *he* wants.

5
The High-Desire Diet

Once every two or three years, somebody publishes a book or a magazine article on "Food That Turns You On." It's usually oysters or peaches or caviar, rarely it's prunes; but the truth of the matter is that *no* food has a directly stimulatory effect on your sexuality. You can eat oysters until they come out of your ears, but apart from filling you up with some useful vitamins and minerals, they will do very little to improve your love life.

Mary Quant, the British dress designer, once said that oysters "are sensuous to eat in themselves—they are like eating people, very much like biting into a person."

I don't know where Mary buys *her* oysters (they don't sound like bluepoints to me), but it would probably be cheaper and sexier (although less nutritious) for her to eschew oysters altogether and bite directly into people.

As I discussed in *How to Drive Your Man Wild in Bed*, men have searched for years for an effective aphrodisiac, some secret pill or powder they can slip into the drink or food of poor unsuspecting women and turn them instantly into insatiable nymphomaniacs. Or, conversely, for women whose sexual appetites are already quite insatiable enough, men have sought some secret pill or powder that can give them the power to make love, hour after hour, night after night, without ever losing their erections.

Unfortunately, no known substances have these effects, either on men or on women. Even alcohol is ineffective because although it can occasionally provoke desire, it usually seriously undermines performance. And no food or potion, however exotic, however rare, has been scientifically observed to turn women into sex-hungry maniacs or men into the genital equivalent of the Washington Monument. Countless rhinoceroses have been slaughtered for their horns; countless ginseng plants uprooted; countless soldier beetles ground up to make Spanish fly; and all to no avail.

The only possible erotic effect that any of these substances might have is psychological: If you *think* they're going to excite you, then they very well might. But if you're considering trying any of them yourself, I would seriously advise you to save your money. I've even seen a "suck-me liquid" on mail-order sale that *absolutely guarantees* that every woman who takes it will immediately want to get her mouth around the penis of the lucky administrator. The ingredients are supposed to include Spanish fly; the price is $25.

In actual fact, real Spanish fly is a harmful irritant that can cause painful swelling of the genitourinary tract and even death. Casanova was said to have given it to two prostitutes, and one of them was in such agony that she threw herself out of an upstairs window. So—even though most "love potions" on sale today are harmless placebos—*never* follow any man's suggestion to try a pill, powder, or liquid that is supposed to turn you on. It could be sugar water, it could be PCP, or it could be something even more dangerous. The only sexual stimulants you need are your mind, your body, and your man.

That isn't to say that a good refreshing diet can't put you into a better mood for love. When you're dating a man with whom you think you may later be doing a little loving, it's worth going easy on the heavy foods and restricting your intake of wine. There are few experiences more uncomfortable than having a 210-pound man bouncing up and down on top of your stomach when you've just eaten a huge bowl of fettucine with clam sauce, followed by guinea fowl with olives, and a large slice of chocolate cake, with five glasses of Chianti and a cup of espresso.

There are certain light foods that are not only healthy and will contribute to your general well-being and therefore to your enjoyment of sex, but that have spices and textures and tastes that make them very complementary to an evening of erotic behavior. Avocados are always good, because they taste rich and sensual while at the same time have a very high vitamin E content, which is beneficial to your sexual health in general and your fertility in particular. Serve the avocados sliced and tossed with a sharp Italian dressing or mixed with mozzarella cheese and slices of tomato.

Shellfish are generally regarded as being good for the libido; and one of my favorite snacks is prawn balls (easy to eat in bed, absolutely delicious, and suggestively named, so you couldn't ask for very much more than that).

Here's what you will need to make prawn balls (Tord Mun Kung):

MORE WAYS TO DRIVE YOUR MAN WILD IN BED • 97

1 lb peeled raw prawns
4 cloves garlic
$\frac{1}{2}$ teaspoon ground black pepper
$\frac{1}{2}$ tablespoon ground coriander root
salt
peanut oil for frying

To make them, chop the prawns finely; then pound together in a mortar the cloves of garlic, adding coriander root, black pepper, and salt to taste. Add the prawns to the mortar, and pound them into a fine paste. Shape the paste into small balls, and deep fry them in peanut oil. You can make prawn balls in advance and refry them at any time to heat them up.

Another delicious food for you and your lover to eat by hand on one of those casual, sensual, anything-goes kind of evenings is *souscaille*, which comes from Martinique, in the Caribbean.

For souscaille sauce, you will need:

$\frac{1}{3}$ pint cold water
2 cloves garlic, crushed
$\frac{1}{2}$ teaspoon salt
3 green chili peppers, finely chopped
3 tablespoons lime juice
freshly ground black pepper

You make a sauce out of the water, garlic, salt, pepper, freshly squeezed lime juice, and green chili peppers. You then sit together and slice fresh green mangoes, marinading each slice in the sauce for at least ten minutes. Then you eat them, voluptuously.

Both the Chinese and the Japanese swear by the

erotic properties of bamboo shoots. My favorite recipe for bamboo shoots is called *kinome no takenoko yaki.*

You will need the following ingredients for sautéed bamboo shoots (kinome no takenoko yaki)

2 bamboo shoots

15 kinome leaves (or small bunch parsley)

¼ cup soy sauce

2 tablespoons mirin

1 tablespoon sake

1 tablespoon oil for frying

To make it first drain and slice the bamboo shoots; then finely chop parsley and *kinome* leaves together and mix them with the soy sauce, *mirin,* and *sake.* Then all you have to do is heat the oil in a pan, toss and fry the bamboo shoots, add the soy and *kinome* mixture, and sautée for a little while. Serve in delicate bowls, decorated with a little more chopped *kinome.*

Many sweet dishes are supposed to have provocative if not actually aphrodisiac qualities. Honey—especially when blended up with a pint of milk, an egg, and a tablespoon of brewer's yeast—is supposed to be an incomparable pick-me-up after a night of loving or a morning of more loving.

One of my favorite puddings for a sexy evening out (or an even sexier evening in) is a Bajan dish from Barbados. It's often called Pitch Lake pudding, because it was supposedly inspired by Trinidad's lake of natural asphalt; although believe me, it tastes a whole lot better. The key to making it taste arousing is the old rum you add as the finishing touch.

Pitch Lake pudding requires the following:

4 ozs unsweetened cocoa
2 tablespoons instant coffee
8 ozs sugar
5 egg yolks
5 egg whites
5 tablespoons dark rum
salt
1/2 pint thick cream

Spoon the cocoa powder into a bowl on top of a pan of hot water (or into the top pan of a double boiler). Then dissolve the instant coffee and sugar into one-fourth pint of boiling water, stirring to make sure that all the sugar has melted. Stir the coffee and sugar mixture a little at a time into the cocoa, and warm it over a low heat for five minutes. Beat in the five egg yolks, one at a time, whipping the mixture furiously after you have added each one. Add a pinch of salt to the five egg whites and beat them until they stand up stiff. Then fold them into the cocoa mixture, thoroughly and sensually. Pour the resulting pudding into a large glass dish, and refrigerate for at least eight hours. Before serving, whip up a half-pint of thick cream with a tablespoonful of sugar and as much dark Barbados *rhum vieux* as you can manage (about three to four tablespoonfuls should do nicely). Spread the rum cream over the mousse, and serve in small glass dishes.

To me, the most erotic foods are the foods that you like the best, carefully prepared and attractively served, with a light and interesting wine to accompany them. As a rule, it's better to avoid red wines on a sexy evening out, not only because they are considerably more fattening than white wines, but because they tend to make you feel very much worse the morning after. And the morning after, you will certainly want to be as fresh and as active as you were the night before . . . as we shall see later on when we talk about how to drive your man wild in bed even when you wake up the following day.

It can occasionally be fun to use food as a sexual seasoning in itself. Several mail-order companies market flavored liquids and creams—mint, strawberry, or banana—for you to rub onto your breasts or vulva to give yourself an interesting taste when your man makes love to you. Or you can use a banana itself, slipped into your vagina, as a stimulating and nourishing treat, to be eaten out of you inch by inch.

Marcia, a law graduate from Philadelphia, told me, "Once, when my boyfriend and I were going to bed together, I made sure that I got into bed before he did, and lay there with my legs apart, and a cocktail cherry just between the lips of my cunt. He was toweling himself off from the shower and talking to me, and then he looked down and saw the cherry, and then he looked me in the eyes, and then he looked back at the cherry, and I said, 'It's yours, go ahead, eat it,' and his cock rose up as if it had been jerked up on a string. He bent down between my legs, even though his hair was still wet, and he licked that cherry out of me, and even when he'd finished eating the cherry, he went on licking and licking, and I have to admit that I loved it."

On the whole, though, food and sex don't mix together particularly well. It's surprising how long it takes a man to eat a banana, especially when he's highly aroused and trying to kiss and lick your vulva at the same time. It's better to use food as an appetizer, rather than as an addition to the main course, except when some really extraordinary sexual idea hits you.

Twenty-one-year-old Debbie, from Indianapolis, explained what she had done with her fiancé Tad. "He came around one morning and my parents were out and I was making pancakes. Tad had promised me the previous evening that he would come by, and I knew he loved pancakes, so that was why I was making them. And sausage links, too. He liked those. Well, anyway, he just sat in the kitchen while I was making the pancakes and then he came up behind me and started putting his arms around me and squeezing my breasts and everything, and I was only wearing my nightdress so pretty soon he was playing with my nipples and running his hand right down between my legs and I was getting very excited. I said I was going to have to stop cooking, I couldn't cook when he was doing that to me. So we went into the living room with a tray of pancakes and maple syrup and sat down on the floor by the coffee table, and then Tad said, 'What am I supposed to do, dip the pancakes into the jug? You didn't bring any plates.' Well, I was about to get some plates, but then I suddenly thought of something else to do, something sexy. I opened up my nightdress and opened up my legs and poured the maple syrup out of the jug onto my stomach, so that it trickled down through my hair and slid into pussy and right down between the cheeks of my bottom. And I said, 'Go ahead—there are the pancakes, here's the syrup. You don't need any plates.' He was kind of hesitant at first, but then he tore off a piece of pancake and dipped it into the syrup on my stomach.

"Then I took hold of his hand and pressed the pancake right in between my legs, and smeared it around and around. He took it and ate it, and all the time he looked at me like you wouldn't believe, like all he could think of was getting me into bed. He ate another pancake, and then he said, 'Who needs pancakes?' and he pushed me back on the rug and he licked the syrup right off my stomach and right out from between my legs, and stuck the tip of his tongue right into my asshole to lick the syrup out of there, too. We made love right there and then on the floor, and we were all sticky and sweaty, and I loved it so much I was kicking my legs and crying out. He took his cock out of me just before he climaxed, and his sperm shot all over my stomach and mixed with the syrup, and I mixed it around some more and wiped it off of myself with my fingers, and licked it, and it was the sweetest-bitterest thing I ever tasted. I guess that was *my* breakfast. Just like he said, 'Who needs pancakes?' "

While sugary treats like Debbie's may give instant energy and excitement, they are positively harmful to the teeth and of course to the waistline. So even if you have a sweet-toothed man, try to save all those puddings and candies for those *very* special occasions. Semen, incidentally, is *not* fattening; not unless it's ingested in *enormous* quantities. It contains nothing more than a little protein and a few simple sugars. And all those myths that you may have heard about it, that it improves your bustline, that it clears your skin, that it regulates your metabolism, are regrettably false. I have come across nine or ten women who regularly insist that their lovers ejaculate onto their faces so that they can smear the semen into their skin to give them an instant face mask; but although it does have a "tightening" effect, I have no scientific evidence that it does them anything but psychological good. We shall talk about the question of swallowing your lover's semen when we discuss the pleasures of oral sex in more detail. Whether or not you decide to make your lover's semen part of your calorie-controlled diet, your eating habits will affect your sex life, and that is why I have drawn up, with the aid of two diet experts, one American and one Chinese, an eating plan that will not deprive you of flavor or satisfaction, but will help you to reach the peak of fitness that energetic and satisfying sex demands.

DAY ONE Breakfast: hot lemon juice, crisp bread with cottage cheese and a slice of lox. Lunch: Chicken breast quickly stir fried with very little oil and one tablespoon soy sauce, green onions, bamboo shoots, and a small cupful of steamed rice; green tea. Dinner: Small mixed salad with lemon juice dressing, white wine spritzer.

DAY TWO Breakfast: Half grapefruit, bran cereal. Lunch: Veal braised in white wine with green beans, mineral water. Dinner: Slices of pear and mozzarella cheese, vinegar dressing, white wine spritzer.

DAY THREE Breakfast: Filet of smoked trout with one scrambled egg cooked with low-fat spread, jasmine tea. Lunch: Thin slice of lean steak, marinated in *sake*, then broiled, with Chinese leaf quick-fried with chopped red chilis, white wine spritzer. Dinner: Cottage cheese and slices of apple, mineral water.

DAY FOUR Breakfast: Hot lemon juice, salad of oranges, grapefruit, and white grapes. Lunch: Cold lean ham with salad of red beans, chopped cucumber, diced pears, mineral water. Dinner: Chicken broth with spring onions.

DAY FIVE Breakfast: Sliced smoked turkey, orange juice. Lunch: White fish filet poached in dry vermouth until tender, broccoli. Dinner: Watermelon slice served with jalapeño pepper dip (you'd be amazed at the stunning taste of it!) white wine spritzer.

You can repeat this diet for two consecutive weeks, but for the third week you should return to eating normally. Thereafter, use it for a week at a time whenever you feel that your body shape is misbehaving itself.

This diet does something that very few diets do. It gives you all the basic nutrition you need, but it gives you varied and stimulating flavors, too. So many high-protein low-caloire diets are bland and tedious, but I insisted when I asked my two experts to prepare a plan that they occasionally sacrifice saving calories in favor of gaining flavor. You won't ever stick to a diet that is boring.

Once you're in shape, of course, you're going to have to find yourself a man to practice on.

6

Coming On Strong—The Secret to Attracting a Man's Attention

One of the advantages of the confidence that today's women display is that it better equips them to meet and attract the men they want. With few exceptions, most men are very much more cautious about approaching women than they like to admit, especially when those women, like you, are especially well-groomed and especially dynamic and have a very, very feminine charisma.

When they meet a woman to whom they're really attracted, most men tend to react in one of these three ways. Either they turn into a high-fat-content Casanova, all droopy lidded and husky voiced and excessively flattering. "Did anybody ever tell you that you have stunning ears? And your neck . . . it's flawless."

Or else they turn into an obnoxious bastard, talking aggressively and insultingly, not just to impress the woman, but also to bring her down to a level at which they feel more able to manage her. Obnoxious bastards always swear a lot and act drunker than they are. "The trouble with snobby women like you, you've all forgotten what it feels like to fuck."

Or else they turn into men of stone, ignoring you completely by striking interesting Clint Eastwood–like poses (notice the cheek muscle twitching slightly *à la A Fistful of Dollars*) in the hope that you will be intrigued by their taciturnity and general air of wounded doom.

If, in spite of all their posturing, you find any of these types physically attractive and you're interested in getting to know them better, then there is a *right* way and a *wrong* way to react to their approaches.

For instance, when the high-fat-content Casanova leans against the doorjamb at a party and starts his oily litany of compliments, do not simper and titter and blush. He is in reality not so much flattering you as trying to make you feel uncomfortable so that he can exert more conversational power over you. Play him at his own game. Say "thank you" nicely when he compliments you, and then compliment him in return. But make sure that your compliment is very slightly two-edged. "As a matter of fact, I was looking at you from across the room and thought what a Hellenic nose you have." He will be flattered that you noticed him, but confused at being complimented in return, and even more confused because he doesn't know whether a Hellenic nose is good or bad. At this moment, you will have the conversational edge, and you can begin to show him that you're interested in him, his career, and his pastimes. Ask him questions and keep on asking him questions. Not only will it help you to find out whether he's the kind of man you *really* want to get to know, but you will have given very little away about yourself.

If a man starts coming on like an obnoxious bastard, then no matter how much his language and his conversation offend you, do not allow yourself to appear shocked and upset. Like the high-fat-content Casanova, unsettling you is his way of getting an advantage over you. No matter how much he sneers and swears, never show that you're anything but bored by childish exhibitions like these, and *never* allow yourself to get drawn into whatever it is that he's arguing about. What he's really arguing about isn't politics or art or anything else—it's *you* and the fact that he finds you attractive and doesn't know any other way of getting through to you. Again, the best offensive is to start asking questions such as, "What do you do for a living?" He will have to halt his harangue in midstream and answer you, particularly since obnoxious bastards always love to talk about themselves. Keep on asking him questions about himself and his work and you'll be amazed how quickly he cools down and starts to sound civilized again. That's when you'll be able to find out whether or not there's an attractive man behind that less-than-attractive mouth; and quite often there is. If you get to know him well, he will look back on that time when he first shouted at you with ever-deepening remorse.

The men of stone are easier to handle, although they may seem intimidating at first. All you have to do is approach them and ask them a ritzy, off-the-cuff question such as, "Did I see you on Tremont Street last week, driving a red Ferrari?" Now that is exactly the sort of question that he *doesn't* want you to ask him, because it has nothing whatsoever to do with how moody he looks. And the odds are that he doesn't own a red Ferrari (unless this is a cocktail party in Malibu). He will have to explain that he actually owns a four-year-old Camaro with a hole in the muffler, and that will immediately put him on the defensive. You can then compliment him a little: "Well, you *look* like the kind of guy who drives a red Ferrari." And then quickly follow that up with a few more questions: simple personal questions like where he lives and what he does for a living. You'll be playing along with him, because he did after all want you to make the first approach and take the responsibility for whatever might happen between you. But all the time you'll have the advantage in the power structure of the conversation, and you'll be able to control just how far you want it to go.

Don't let men take over the conversation until you're sure that they've settled down, that they've stopped being excessively oily or absurdly aggressive or stoic to the point of petrification, and that you're sure you like them enough to want to listen to everything they're dying to tell you, like how terrific they are at backgammon and what they think about the Middle Eastern conflict.

The secret of catching and keeping the attention of the man you want is to pluck up your courage and *come on strong*. Men are aroused by women who are positive and outspoken and opinionated. They're a challenge; a conquest worth having, especially when at the same time they are actually relieving the man of a large part of the arduous and intimidating duty of having to woo them and coax them and encourage them. Forget everything you've read about men being frightened by today's decisive, liberated ladies. They're not frightened at all; they love you.

One of the most successful characters I ever created in a thriller wasn't a shy, retiring young girl with batting eyelids and a breathy voice, but an Amazon called Nadine, whom I described as follows:

"She was 5 feet 10 inches, with thick wavy brunette hair, shoulders like Arnold Schwarzenegger and a magnificent 38-inch bust. Somebody had once said that she would look better as the figurehead for a ship."

Nadine, who appeared in my recent novel *Ikon*, was commanding, intolerant, and treated all the men around her like minions. Yet the response I received from male readers who instantly fell in love with her was astonishing. One middle-aged man I knew was so stricken by her that he frustratedly accused me of knowing who she was and where she was and of deliberately withholding her whereabouts from him.

Again and again in men's erotic fiction it is the woman who takes charge of the sexual situation. In a famous Victorian story, *La Rose d'Amour*, we meet Manette, who comes into our innocent hero's bedchamber and says, " 'I have something to show you that will please and satisfy you much more than your mistress could do.'

"I followed her to her chamber, which after entering, she locked. I stood looking out of a window while Manette went behind the bed, the curtains of which were drawn. Hearing a light step advancing towards me I turned round and Manette stood before me entirely naked; she sprung into my arms, clasping me round the neck, and led me to the bed, on which she seated herself.

"I threw off my coat and vest while she let down my pantaloons and drew out my blunt but ever ready weapon, then falling back on the bed, drew me on top of her. My cock soon ran its full length into the soft and luscious sheath which nature had intended for it. Twice before I got off her did I open the floodgates of love's reservoir, and pour into her a stream of fiery sperm, as each time she met me, letting down the very cream and essence of her body so copiously that our thighs were bedewed with it."

And so on, and so on! But it is very interesting to note that "our hero," for all of his thrusting and for all of his floodgate opening, did nothing to create or control the sexual encounter. It was the girl who invited him into her room and even took down his trousers for him. None of the responsibility for the encounter was his. And this active-woman/passive-man scenario is repeated so often in both pornographic and respectable fiction that it can be seen to represent with some accuracy the strong underlying need that men feel for women who are interested in them to approach them positively, even domineeringly.

"Martin had only to wait for a few moments before the front door was opened, and Eugenie appeared. She looked striking. Her hair had been swept back, and she was wearing a white silk robe trimmed with marabou.

"'Are you ready?' he asked her, bowing. 'The table is booked for nine o'clock.'

"But without a word, Eugenie opened her robe, and displayed to Martin that she was completely naked underneath. Her nipples stiffened in the cool evening wind, but she made no move back inside. Still saying nothing, she took Martin's hand, and placed it on her breast.

"'Does that excite you?' she said, at last.

"Martin could scarcely find the words to reply. Eugenie took his hand again, and moved it down so that it was pressed against her pubic hair. 'Would you do anything for me?' she asked him. Martin nodded, and said, 'You know that I would.'

"'In that case,' said Eugenie, 'you must insert one single finger into my vagina, as far as it will go, and you must turn it around three times, and say the magic words, I am your slave, and then you must withdraw your finger and touch it to your lips, to prove that you are mine.'"

That scene comes from *Under Pink Skies*, the classic French erotic memoir by Eugenie Eclat, in which Eugenie herself always plays the dominant role.

These are very blatantly sexual examples, but the

male sexual psychology that they reveal remains the same even in less overtly erotic encounters. Men display considerable strength and fortitude in most areas of their lives—in work, in sport, in war. But when it comes to their sexual relationships with women, they evince not so much a lack of confidence but a need for regular reassurance and continual response. It is in sex that true equality lies; and no matter what feminists might say about the kind of stories that I have just quoted, they are to me evidence not of men's feelings of disrespect for women or of superiority over them, but of their dependence on women to participate strongly and actively in sexual relationships and of the importance they attach to receiving from women a very strong and clear response to every sexual move they make, from a cocktail-party conversation to the stimulation of their clitorises.

How many times have you heard the accusation from a man that his wife or lover is frigid and unresponsive? The woman may be enjoying her sex life thoroughly, but good sex depends not so much on mutual enjoyment but mutual communication of that enjoyment. The familiar catch phrases show clearly how much anxiety buzzes around in a man's mind not just from giving his lover a good time but from *knowing* that he has given her a good time. "Was it good for you, darling?" "Did the earth move?"

This anxiety begins at the very first encounter, and that is why so many men respond in the ways that I mentioned at the beginning of this chapter. They start to play a complicated kind of power politics, so that they can feel in charge of the situation, or at least so that they can induce you to take charge of the situation without making themselves appear weak.

You, of course, will have all of your own anxieties,

which are largely a mirror-image of his: How can I make him notice me? Will he think I'm being boring? Does he think I look attractive? Perhaps he thinks I'm coming on too strong? Why do I keep laughing in that inane way?

But if you understand what it is that a man is looking for when he meets you and feels attracted to you—a positive, almost blatant sign that you find him attractive, and that you are prepared to consider more advances from him—then you will find that more often than not you will have surprising success. Men are not particularly subtle creatures, and so too much sexual subtlety tends to be lost on them. I knew a girl who spent an entire evening with a man she adored, trying to be mysterious and alluring and unapproachable, while all the time she was quivering with desire for him. At the end of the evening he simply drove her home, pecked her on the cheek, said, "Sorry it hasn't been a very exciting evening," and left her on the doorstep feeling utterly deflated and frustrated.

The trouble was, she had given him no unequivocal signal that he had aroused her interest; she had played out the female equivalent of the men of stone, and he had simply taken her act at its face value and felt that he was boring her.

When you meet a man you like, you can give him a positive sexual signal first of all by showing a conversational interest in him, by questioning him about his interests. I have yet to meet the man who doesn't respond to being asked questions about his work and his hobbies. Then you can show your *continuing* interest by asking him to do things for you—fetch you a drink, button up your dress at the back, find you a chair—actions that will increase his sense of possessiveness about you.

Once you have managed to arouse his possessiveness, you are almost home free. He will guard you against the approach of other men and feel increasingly better toward you if you make it clear that you and he are together. There is nothing better guaranteed to boost a man's ego and his sexual interest in you than having to fight for you, provided he always wins.

This technique can work just as effectively on your husband or live-in lover and can serve to restimulate his interest in you after years of familiarity. When you go to a party or social function, act as if you were 17 years old, out on your first date, and behave toward your husband or lover in a specially admiring way. Again, ask him some questions about himself; don't assume that just because you've been living with him for five years you know everything about him. Ask him what he thinks about the party, about the woman with the big breasts sitting on the other side of the room, about today's politics, about you, about everything and anything. And *listen* to what he says. Do some small, intimate thing for him, like brushing his hair away from his ear; touch him; kiss him from time to time; simply make him feel that you're still interested in him sexually, that he has a sexual charisma that attracts you. Tell him about yourself, how you feel, how much you love him. And remember, no matter how long you've been together, never ever take him for granted.

Norma, 28, tried this conversational technique on her husband David at their annual company celebration in Toledo, Ohio. She told me afterward, "I thought I knew what kind of a man David was. Safe, reliable, honest, pretty unexciting. But all evening I made a point of showing him that I was his, that he was interesting; and when we returned home that night he took me straight up to the bedroom, carried me up, and undressed me, and made love to me better than at any time since we first met. He was so good: He was strong, he was confident, he aroused me so much. We spent the rest of the night talking—talking till dawn, and we found out things about each other and the way we felt that we'd never even shared. We'd been living two separate lives, mentally and sexually, and it took one of us to break it down and say, 'Hey, what goes on here? We're supposed to love each other, let's start *really* loving each other.'"

"By the way," she said, "thank you." For Norma had written to me for advice after reading *How to Drive Your Man Wild in Bed*, and that was the advice that I had given her.

We are talking about the same thing we discussed at the very beginning of this book—communication: sharing feelings, sharing fantasies, sharing fears, sharing experiences. Sex is a means of communication but not a complete one, not for the complex burden of emotions and anxieties and questions that every human encounter, especially a sexual encounter, carries with it. Talking always helps; in fact, you can never do too much talking, especially to the one you love.

When you start talking to a man who attracts you, you can use all kinds of body language to reinforce the signals that you're sending him. You can lean closer, crossing your legs; you can touch his shoulder, or affectionately squeeze his thigh if he says something that amuses you; you can whisper in his ear; if you're standing next to him at a cocktail-party circle, you can stand closely behind him, so that your breast brushes against his arm. He'll feel it, don't worry; and even if he's not sure that you did it on purpose, it'll arouse him. When he's talking to you, look directly and unswervingly into his eyes, and hold your head in your hands the way that he would do if he were about to kiss you.

I am frequently asked by women about dress.

What should I wear when I go out to attract a man? Because in spite of their natural dress sense, many women are not sure whether a dress that is lowcut and slinky is going to attract the man they want or put him off; or whether a sensible pair of pants and a country-cousin blouse is going to look frumpy or smart. How does a man react to what I wear?

There are two main points to remember about dressing to seduce. One is that some dresses are just too sexy for some men. They like to be aroused, but they also feel insecure if every other man in the room is staring down the cleavage of the girl they consider to be "theirs." By this, I am not suggesting for a moment that you should restrain your dress just to satisfy the territorial instincts of the man you want to attract but that you do not need to kill a duck with an elephant gun. If you like to wear see-through gowns that show your nipples, then wear see-through gowns that show your nipples. But consider at the same time the effect on the man you're after. Can he handle that kind of stress at a time when he's trying to act strong and confident and seductive, too?

There does come a point at which a dress that is obviously meant to attract and flatter the man that you're with becomes publicly rather than privately exhibitionistic. Movie stars like Barbra Streisand and pop stars like Cher make regular appearances in black clingy evening dresses that show off their bare breasts beneath. But they are movie stars, and even though there are plenty of beautiful and filmy blouses and gowns these days that give more than a subtle hint of nipple, a shadowy outline of breast, how far *you* go is up to your own judgment and the age and taste and background of your lover to be. Provoke him, but think about the possibility that you may disconcert him. On the other hand, he may not give a damn. He may be the kind of man who loves to have a woman on his arm whose near nudity makes whole restaurants turn and stare, in which case, all you have to think about is, is it going to be chilly tonight?

Seductiveness in clothing, however, doesn't always or necessarily mean near nudity. A woman who is beautifully and simply dressed in very feminine clothes can look far more alluring than a woman who is dressed in a plunging evening gown. A silk blouse worn without a bra can look stunningly erotic. A headscarf, a skirt, a pair of well-cut pants, can all give you far more magic than the sexiest dress. Have your hair done well, pay attention to your makeup, wear an expensive and subtle perfume, and you will have him eating out of your hand, or anywhere else you care to have him eat.

Also, as your affair or your marriage progresses, pay attention from time to time to those sexy little ways of dressing and undressing that *appear* unconscious but that can refresh his interest in you like 110 volts of electricty.

Michelle, 23, has been married for two years to Dan, her advertising executive husband, and, generally, she says, their marriage is full of pep. "But I know he likes it when I come into his den when he's working to bring him a drink or a cup of coffee and I'm wearing nothing but a pair of jeans. It makes him feel that I'm still out to turn him on; which I am. He always gets up from his desk and kisses me and starts playing with my breasts, but I always say, come on now, get back to your work. Later, though, when he's finished, he's always charged up and very ready to go."

Adana, 27, from Boston, Massachusetts, had what she called "the sexiest day of my life" when she and her boyfriend set out to decorate their apartment. Giving her boyfriend the excuse that she didn't want to spoil any of her clothes, Adana painted the living room nude except for a thong and a headscarf. "Jim was supposed to be painting the kitchen, but he kept coming in to see how I was doing. Soon he came up and put his arms around me, and then he started kissing me and caressing me all over. I was holding a dripping paint-roller in my hand, and we began to get smothered in yellow paint. Jim stripped off his T-shirt and jeans, and he was as hard as a brush handle. I couldn't touch him, I had too much paint on my hands, so I knelt down on the floor in front of him and began to lick at him with my tongue, so that his cock bobbed up and down. Then I took him into my mouth and slowly started to suck him. He pushed me gently back onto the floor, and we made love in a whole slippery mess of paint. And we kept on doing it again and again, all day. I think we must have made love five times before it began to grow dark, and all we'd managed to paint was half of one wall. And *ourselves*, of course. But sometimes you need a day like that; a day of total sex; a day of total self-indulgence, and I think that the woman can initiate it just as easily as the man."

As we said, coming on strong in the way you dress needn't necessarily involve nudity, or even seminudity. Several women I talked to reported rousing success with the man they wanted to attract with miniskirts, battle dress blousons unbuttoned just *one* button lower than usual, tightly fitting pedal pushers, or anything striking and attractive and noticeable.

All in all, be positive, both in your approaches to men and in the way you look when you make them. The days of the shy and retiring young lady are over, and there are very few men who regret their passing. A woman who speaks for herself and grooms herself well will get any man she wants and will get any man excited.

7

Sex and the New You

You will have noticed that throughout the course of this book I have emphasized again and again the active part that you can play in making your sex life informed, interesting, and exciting. I have assumed right from the beginning that you are an intelligent, alert women who is not shocked by the frank discussion of sexual activities. And I have also assumed that you want an even more exciting sex life, which is why you picked up this book in the first place.

So many sex books for women these days still retain that coy, medicinal approach of the 1960's, as if they had been written all the way through in breathy, patronizing tones. "Well, dear, about your clitoris . . ." But the reality of today's women is that they are completely explicit about what they expect from their sex lives, and they are willing to discuss in the plainest of terms what they can do to achieve more pleasure, more satisfaction, and a far closer relationship with the men they love.

All the same, you do have your reservations and your sensitivities, as everybody does when it comes to sex, and you should expect your husband or lover to be alert to whatever needs and anxieties you feel. Just because you have been learning how to take a more positive role in your sex life, it doesn't mean for a moment that your man can lie back and let you do all the work. You should expect him to respond to your sexual assertiveness by being even more sexually assertive himself and by rewarding your efforts to give him the time of his life in kind.

You should expect him to understand, too, that you may not be enthusiastic about certain sexual practices—that some sexual variations may not appeal to you at all—and that even though you have agreed to share your body with him for the purposes of mutual communication and the sharing of affection, ultimately your body is yours and is to be respected, just as you respect his. You are your own woman, and what you give to him you give out of choice, and that is its value.

Here's Nicola, now 33, a one-time nude model from Dallas, Texas: "I met Bob at a discotheque in Fort Worth, when I was home visiting my parents. He was straightforward, strong, very masculine, and he was about 6 feet 6 inches tall, so he made me feel very feminine and protected. His father owned a spread just outside of Fort Worth, and that weekend he drove me out there and showed me the farm and introduced me to all of his family. Then, after supper, he took me out to his cottage on the grounds, and played a couple of records, and started kissing me and sliding his hand inside of my shirt. I said, 'Hold on, Bob, I *like* you, but I'm not at all sure that I want to go straight into a sexual relationship, particularly after nothing much more than three kisses and a meal with your mom.' He was really angry.

"He said, 'You showed your body off to all those men in those magazines, and now you're quibbling about going to bed with me.' And I said, 'What's the matter with you, just because I showed them my body doesn't mean to say that I'm immoral or anything. I didn't go to bed with any of them, not one of them, not even the photographer, not even the magazine's publisher, and *that* took some doing. So don't go thinking that I jump into bed with every cowboy who picks me up at a disco.' Well, I'm not sure I should have said that. It was kind of insulting. And he saw it as a challenge, too. He tore off my shirt, and then he ripped off my slacks, and I wasn't wearing a bra, so all I was left with was see-through panties. He pushed me back on the couch, and opened up his jeans, and his cock was rearing up like one of those stallions of his.

"I suppose I was afraid, and that made it look bigger, but I won't ever forget the way it looked: thick and crimson and threatening. He sat on top of me, straddled me, you know; and he pushed his cock between my breasts, and then up against my mouth. I was frightened then. I won't pretend that I wasn't aroused, because I was. I did like him, and if he'd behaved different, I would have gone to bed with him anyway. But it was the way he took it for granted that he was going to fuck me that put me off. Well, I guess my decision was that it was safer to go along with it than risk getting hurt. I opened my mouth and sucked his cock, and it was a real mouthful. I was getting turned on but I was angry, too, and I don't see contradiction in that; a man can force himself on you and turn you on and afterwards just because you were sexually excited he thinks that everything's okay, that he's forgiven. But it isn't, and he's not."

I can't imagine how many times that must happen during marriages, but the point about it is that no man can expect to treat a woman as something he can use for his own sexual gratification whenever he feels like it; and just because his woman decides not to fight him and risk getting herself hurt, just because he fucks her and she reaches an orgasm, that in itself is not a credential for boorish and disrespectful behavior. Anyway, Bob fucked me in the mouth, right down my throat, and then he fucked my cunt; and he really rammed himself into me as if he wanted to hurt me. I didn't know whether I was going to cry or climax. Then he turned me over, and he pushed himself right up my bottom, and that hurt, terribly, but it gave me an orgasm straight away, even though it hurt, and Bob came too, right up inside my bottom.

"After that, as soon as I was able to, I got dressed and asked Bob to drive me back to Forth Worth. He said, 'Why? I thought we were enjoying ourselves.' I said, 'The day you grow up, and stop treating women as if they were cows and you were the stud bull, then you'll understand why.' Now, the thing about it is, if I'd tried to report Bob for rape, you can imagine what kind of a deal I would have gotten in court. Because if I had laid my hand on the Bible and had to answer the question 'Did you enjoy it?' I would have truthfully have had to say 'Yes, I did.' I liked Bob very much, physically and as a friend, and when he fucked me like that I was excited. In fact, I liked it a lot, and I sound now as if I'm complaining unnecessarily. But I didn't actually want to go to bed with him that night, and if I'd been physically stronger I wouldn't have. And it's my feeling that every woman has a right to say no and mean it. It's a very hard question. But that incident left me with two thoughts, you know? One was that men ought to be told more about women; and the other was that women ought to be told more about men."

The way that women are depicted in fiction, in films, and even in advertising is still a strong source of irritation to the feminist movement; and in many cases rightly so. But the sexual issues involved are very complicated, because while a war may be going on, there has never been a war in which the combatants are so strongly attracted to one another and in which victory for either side would mean defeat for both. To me, one of the most important steps forward over the past ten years has been the gradual realization by women that they have a right to expect all the sexual gratification that their minds and their bodies can afford them and that their husbands or lovers have an obligation to help them fulfill that right.

Ten years ago, the findings of Masters and Johnson on the subject of female orgasm were just becoming widely recognized enough for women to understand that orgasm was not just an expectation but an integral part of their everyday sexual enjoyment.

Now, women have the social and emotional potential to get what they want; not necessarily by strident demands and certainly not by alienating men by denouncing their sexual fantasies. (Has it ever occurred to you that *Playboy* doesn't degrade women—if anything, it overexalts them?) And that is why, in this book, I have addressed the pleasures and problems of driving your man wild in bed in a far more open and positive way; maybe a less compromising way, too. Unlike the ladies of ten years ago, I expect you to know what you want, and I also expect you to have faith in your ability to play a full and demanding role in your love affair.

As we have seen from Nicola's experience, however, there are still difficulties when it comes to dealing with the practice rather than the theory. There are still plenty of men out there who see women as sex objects; not even nicely, not even as pinups or glamor girls, but as erotic creatures that are designed for their sexual pleasure and for nothing else. Nicola's experience is repeated time and time again, thousands of times, every day and every night, all across America. In its meanest and least objectionable manifestation, it takes the form of a husband who has forgotten to care about his wife, sticking himself up her and then falling asleep. In the most insidious forms, it takes the form of near rape, like Nicola's, or sadism, or woman beating. In any form, the man fails to act like a responsible adult.

A man has a duty to please, to satisfy, and to care for the woman with whom he is having a sexual relationship. The sharing of bodies and the sharing of erotic delights is not just a mechanical process—not what one eighteenth-century cynic called "the voluptuous friction of two intestines."

So how do you get your man to understand your needs and your feminine integrity? How do you guide him so that he doesn't feel that you're trying to take charge of your relationship, so that he doesn't feel unmanly or diminished?

The first thing to do is to be frank. If a man is genuinely interested in you, he won't be put off by a polite refusal to go to bed with him. He'll try again, and he'll respect you more for making him wait. I know this sounds like old-fashioned advice, but it's remarkable how many men are still trying the old-fashioned ploys. "If you love me, prove it," and other similar old chestnuts.

When you go out with a man for the first time and you arouse him, he'll feel very frustrated both socially and sexually that you don't agree to go to bed with him. Just as a man gets the most pleasure out of the very first spurt of semen he climaxes, he gets intense pleasure out of having sex with a girl the very first time he meets her or dates her. It's nothing psychologically complicated. It's simply that it gives him a feeling of having conquered you by sheer looks and charm and charisma, instead of having had to work at it. You, in return, should be flattered that he wants to go to bed with you straight away. But your psychology is different from his. You want to be wooed, to be persuaded, to be made to feel that your body has some value.

He won't think you're cheap if you go to bed with him the very first time you meet him, but the problem is that you might. You may also find that you have slightly lost the upper hand on your relationship, because the next time you meet he will want to make love to you again, probably straight away, and the second time it will be a great deal more difficult for you to say no.

I'm not saying that you should always refuse to have sex with a man on your first date with him; quite often you'll really feel that you want to. But if you're not sure or you think that he's not treating you with sufficient care and respect, then ignore all of those fancy arguments of his, ignore the gibes you might get, too, and say no. Say I like you; say I think you're sexy; say maybe next time; but unless you're sure of him, say no.

If he's angry, which he very well might be—even if he's very fond of you—then don't take it too seriously. Stay calm: It's only the seminal fluid talking down there in his groin in his urethral bulb, bursting to get itself squirted out. That feeling can make a man feel really ratty for just a short while; but if you calm him down, he'll gradually return to normal. Mind you, if he *stays* angry, then you only have one option, and that's to walk out.

Just remember: When you date a man, you have no responsibility to empty his seminal fluid for him. If he finds the frustration overwhelming, tell him you're flattered, but that until you're ready to start a sexual relationship with him, he's going to have to wait.

To regain the sexual attention of a man with

whom you have been living and making love for a long time, your husband, or your live-in lover, you're going to have to work a slightly different way. Start dressing differently; start smartening yourself up more often; go out more, even if it's just to talk to neighbors; make yourself look like an independent lady. You'd be surprised how often your efforts to look independent will bear fruit in helping you to *be* independent. Jan, a 35-year-old housewife from New Milford, Connecticut, said, "Peter is a great guy, good looking, humorous, and I know that he loves me. But about two years ago I really began to feel that he was taking me for granted. He didn't see me as sexy anymore. He didn't see me as attractive or alluring. We still made love, but not very frequently, and even though we had an occasional 'session' as we called it, when we really indulged ourselves sexually for two or three hours, the rest of our sex life was pretty routine. I guess I just decided that I'd had enough.

"All I did was go out and buy myself a small new wardrobe of clothes. Slightly younger clothes, though not *too* young. Then I took to driving around visiting my friends, getting involved in local social events, going to aerobics classes. I got myself elected onto one or two committees. Suddenly I was *me*, not just Peter's wife, and I think he sensed the difference in me because he started paying more attention to what I said and what I thought.

"I felt better. I felt sexier, in the sense that I felt like more of a woman, instead of an accouterment. And along with my new feeling of well being, Peter began to treat me with more respect and to *seduce* me rather than just exercise his marital rights.

"One night I came home and I couldn't believe my eyes. Peter had cooked dinner, veal parmigiana, and set the table with candles, and he was so romantic and loving to me that we ended up having the evening of our lives. It was even better than our honeymoon. He made love to me for hours. He kissed me, and carressed my breasts, and stimulated me with his tongue. I wasn't counting the climaxes I had, but they came one after another, I never seemed to stopped climaxing.

"The wonderful thing about it was that he regained his own respect in himself as a lover, as well as regaining his respect for me. As far as I can see, what makes sex sexy is the way in which somebody you respect, and somebody who respects you in return, completely gives their body and soul to you. But the respect has to come first, otherwise whatever happens afterwards is meaningless."

Jan managed to alter the course of her marriage and her sex life without antagonizing her husband and without making him feel that she was "taking over." But what do you do if the man you're living with is impossibly macho, thinks that the little woman's place is in the home, and believes that men are in charge of sex and that's all there is to it? Let's face it, even quite lovable men can behave like that. Sometimes you love them because they behave like that. But you're not going to be able to get the best out of your sex life if you allow him to dominate your relationship.

Surprisingly, the best way to deal with a man like this is to give him what he wants—in face, too much of what he wants. You will remember from the last chapter, when we discussed the male sexual organs, that after climaxing, men lose interest in sex very promptly and can even find the direct stimulation of their genitals to be irritating and unpleasant.

Of course, your *instinctive* feminine reaction to a domineering man is to say no to him. But if you say yes, and yes, and yes again— if, in fact, you demand that he should satisfy you—you will be surprised how quickly he is prepared to shift his position, and accommodate your needs, both sexually and emotionally. What you will be doing is playing on his inability to produce erection after erection. You will be showing him that men have their weaknesses, just as women do. Unfair? Maybe. But provided you don't allow yourself to be tempted to use his male weakness against him, provided you don't in any way humiliate him, you will find that your revelation of his Achilles heel will go a long way to bringing him into line, no matter how macho he is.

Here's Jane, 24, from Providence, Rhode Island, who had written to me complaining that her boyfriend Chas (a live-in lover of three years) was almost impossibly macho. He treated her and talked about her in front of their friends as if she belonged to him, like a dog, or a snazzy piece of video equipment. He made love to her when he felt like it and didn't when he didn't, and all in all he was a handsome, terrific, *potentially* nice guy but he just didn't understand what it took to make a woman feel happy and respected; or himself, for that matter.

Jane's first instinct was to deny him sex or even to walk out on him for a while and let him see what life was like without her. But she loved him, and she didn't want to risk losing him to some other lady who might be prepared to put up with all of his boorishness.

My suggestion to Jane was that she should suppress her natural instinct to withhold sex, and do just the opposite. As soon as Chas got home at night, she should start kissing him and fondling him and suggest that they go straight to bed together. She should make a special effort to cater to whatever erotic fantasies he had. She should initiate lovemaking between them every single night and every single morning and often wake him up in the middle of the night caressing his penis and demanding that he satisfy her. After lovemaking, she should continue to stimulate him, either manually or orally, and on the whole make him realize that she had her sexual tastes and appetites, too, and that his maleness didn't qualify him to treat her as if she were a receptacle for his occasional bouts of lust.

I told Jane that it was important that she didn't make Chas feel inadequate, even when he might fail to satisfy her. She knew that it was impossible for a man to keep his erection up time and time again; she knew too that she was using that unavoidable physiological fact as something of a weapon against Chas in order to make him understand that she was an individual with tastes and appetites of her own and that she no longer wanted to be treated as Chas's personal property. But she also understood that a man needs his sexual pride. However feminists may gnash their teeth, pride in their ability to satisfy women (however misplaced that pride may sometimes be) is essential to men's sexual performance.

Said Jane, "As soon as Chas got home from a game of golf, I kissed him and made a fuss over him and started squeezing his cock through his pants. He said, 'Heyyy, let me get myself a beer first; but I said, 'Come on, you don't need a beer half as much as I need you.' And do you know something? He wasn't prepared for this. But he couldn't say that he didn't want to fuck me; that would have made him look as if he couldn't do it, or didn't want to do it, so he followed me into the bedroom and I let down my jeans and showed him my cunt.

"Now, I'd always known that he had a fantasy about women with all of their pubic hair shaved off, and so that's what I'd done; I'd shaved all of my pubic hair off so that my cunt was completely bare. He took one look at it and then I really had him under my thumb. All he wanted to do was get me into bed and touch my cunt and suck it; he took the whole of my cunt into his mouth and sucked it, and thrust his tongue right up my vagina; then he tugged down his golfing pants and he fucked me, just the way he always fucked, quickly and rather violently; but after he'd climaxed, I kept on caressing him and kissing him and nibbling him, and I slid right down the bed and took his penis into my mouth. I quite liked it, if you want to know the truth. For the first time I actually felt as if I had *him* in my power instead of the other way around. His penis was soft and still sticky from making love, and when I sucked it gently there was still sperm in it. I could feel Chas go tense; I know that he was feeling too sensitive to be sucked, but, of course, I was out to prove something to him. He said, 'No, no,' but when I looked up and said, 'What is it?' he said, 'It's all right, go on.' He was too macho to say that he couldn't take any more, not just for the moment. Anyway I sucked him and rubbed him and slowly he began to get another erection. It wasn't a particularly hard one, but I sat on top of him and guided him into my cunt, and made him fuck me again. And after about five or ten minutes he managed to reach another climax, even though he was all tensed up and red in the face. I had an orgasm myself, sort of a quiet ripply one, and normally I would have been satisfied, but I went down on him again and licked his cock, and pushed my finger up his ass, and even though he was really doing his best to be sexy, he couldn't handle any more. He said he needed a drink and he got up and fixed us both a vodka tonic.

"I didn't leave him alone that night. Round about three in the morning, I started to press my shaved cunt up against his thigh and massage his cock. He said, 'Oh, no, darling, not again,' but I kept on rubbing him and teasing him and in the end he made love to me—very groggily—but he managed it.

"The next morning I started again, and then he got angry. He asked me what the matter was. I said that I felt like making love to him, that was all. But if he didn't want to . . .

"Gradually, over three or four weeks, our relationship changed. Chas started working harder to make me feel satisfied, and he also started treating me better when we were in company. I think he realized that he had a woman on his hands whom he couldn't control; he couldn't just snap his fingers and expect me to do what he wanted. I managed to change him not by running away from him; the minute you start running away, the minute you try to keep your legs closed and say that he's not getting what he wants, that's the time when you start to admit that you're scared and you're alienated, and all that does is put you more and more into the wrong, at least as far as your partner's concerned. And that just gives him an excuse for treating you worse, and blaming you for everything that goes wrong in your relationship, every argument and every problem. I faced up to my problem with Chas and I won him over, and I'm really glad about that. I got the man I love, as well as the respect I think I deserve. Apart from that, I still enjoy the sex we have these days. Oh, and I still shave my cunt. He really likes that."

The way you think about yourself sexually is also very important to the success of your sexual relationships. You ought to be thinking about yourself more often—your sexual fantasies, your sexual desires, and your sexual responses. That is why I recommend those quiet times on your own, away from your lover or away from your husband, when you take off all of your clothes, give yourself a bath or a shower, and lie back on your bed or couch and touch yourself—not necessarily masturbating, if you don't want to, but putting yourself into a frame of mind when you can think over all of those things that you want out of your sexual relationships.

Marianne, a 31-year-old manager at a dry-cleaning store near La Jolla, California, told me, "Wednesday afternoon is my only free afternoon. My husband is at work, the housework's all done, the store is closed. I use that Wednesday afternoon to take care of myself; to wash my hair, to polish my nails, to wax my legs, to do all of those things that make me a woman. I'm not ashamed of any of those things; I don't think you have to have hairy legs to prove that you're an independent spirit. In any case, I enjoy being groomed and clean and perfumed, I enjoy it for myself.

"I always tell myself every Wednesday afternoon that I'm not going to masturbate, but I always do, and you can tell that I'm not ashamed of it because I'm talking about it now. I told my husband Donald that I did it, about four years ago, and he doesn't mind. He knows that it isn't a substitute for love-making; in fact he knows that it improves my sexuality. Sometimes I use a Coke bottle or a shampoo bottle, but usually I use my fingers. I sit on the floor in front of the wardrobe mirror and I open up my legs and just do it. I fantasize. Of course, I fantasize. I think about all of these men who are watching me do it. I think about men making love to me, ten or eleven men, one after the other, and I push the bottles up my vagina and rub my clitoris, and it only takes four or five minutes before I have an orgasm. The point is, I know what makes me reach a climax, I know what turns me on; and I've explained it to Donald. He respects my fantasies, the same way that I respect his. He has fantasies about fucking me out in the open air, and we've done that two or three times, out in the yard at night, and out on the beach. Whatever he wanted to do, I wouldn't make a fuss about it. The same way, I think he ought to respect what I want out of sex, and he does."

Probably the greatest sexual advance of the past ten years has been the recognition by women like you that you are sexual people, with your own sexual identity, and that you are entitled not only to explore that sexuality as deeply as you want to, but that you can freely enlist the help of your lovers or husbands in achieving satisfaction. This advance has not been accompanied by the media fanfare that made the so-called "Permissive Society" a social and promotional phenomenon in the 1960's. It has happened through the gradual liberalization of movies and magazines and videos, through the growing up of a generation of men and women whose parents have been far less repressive about sex than the previous generation, and through the demands of feminists to know more about their own sex and what they should expect out of their relationships. The result in any case has been that most women now know what they want out of their sex lives, even if they are not entirely sure how to get it.

Ten years ago, when I was preparing *How to Drive Your Man Wild in Bed*, several women asked me whether it was "all right" for women to expect to have regular climaxes. Many women had never experienced a climax and didn't even know what they were. Today, at least, women like you are aware of your sexual entitlement and are prepared to do whatever you can to achieve it.

Ask not what your lover can do for you; ask instead what you can do for each other, and how you can make sure that it happens.

Here's Lilian, 36, talking about her husband Allen: "Our sex life was routine to the point of nonexistence. Once a week, if I was really lucky. Twice a month was more usual, and then it was completely silent, and uninspiring. I don't know why I didn't do something about it sooner, but I guess in a peculiar sort of a way I was afraid. I think many women are. They don't want to hurt their husbands' pride. They don't want them to get angry. But a girlfriend of mine lent me a sexy book called *Delta of Venus* and I began to fantasize about some of the scenes in it and get quite excited. So that day when Allen came home from the office, I was waiting for him naked, wearing nothing but white stockings and a garter belt. He was confused at first and a little embarrassed, but I coaxed him upstairs and into the bedroom and undressed him. I told him I loved him, and that I wanted more of him. I told him how much he excited me, and that we ought to make love all the time, just like we used to on our honeymoon. He kissed me back and began to get fantastically turned-on. He said that he loved making love to me, but somehow he had gotten the idea that I didn't like it too much anymore; he always had the feeling when he made love to me that he was 'pestering' me.

"I couldn't believe what Allen was saying, but I suddenly realized that he had been looking at our routine sex life from a completely different point of view. Neither of us had been telling the other how we felt; and so I'd gradually begun to think that he wasn't particularly interested in making love, and he'd gradually begun to think the same thing about me. Anyway, I lay back and I opened my legs up for him, and he did something he had never ever done before in all the time we'd been married, and that is he licked me between the legs with his tongue. And after what I'd been reading in that *Delta of Venus* book I felt so excited that I had a climax, and then another, one after the other like a ripple that went **right through me.**

"Then Allen climbed onto me and this time I took his cock in my hand and guided it into me. He was good; he was really good; he was as good as I had remembered he was before we started taking each other for granted. He made love to me long and slow, teasing me and tantalizing me, nearly taking his cockhead out of me until I was begging him to push it in, begging him to push in deeper. And then at last he started these strong, thrusting strokes, and I felt as if he were pushing up right inside my stomach, and I had a whole series of little climaxes. At last I could feel him tighten, and he said, 'I can't hold it any more,' and he shot himself into me, so much of it that I could feel it filling me up. I almost blacked out. I opened my eyes and found myself clinging to him, and I could hardly remember what day it was or what time it was or even who I was. All I knew was that I felt very good, and that I loved Allen very much. But I can tell you something, after that day he respected me more; he always treated me better, talked to me more, took an interest in me. I think every woman should realize that a really good sex life is sometimes up to them, too."

8

Sexual Fantasy: The Possible Daydream

Every sexually active man and woman has sexual fantasies of greater or lesser intensity. Some people conjure up erotic fantasies in their minds only when they make love; others spend a large part of their time pursuing one particular fantasy, almost to the point where it becomes the principal interest in their lives.

What I want to show you in this chapter is how you can use your own sexual fantasies to refresh and revitalize your love life and how you can share your fantasies with the man you love. Not *all* of them, necessarily, because fantasies can go way beyond the limits of what your man may consider acceptable—not in the moral sense, but in the sense that your deepest darkest turn-on may have the opposite effect on him than it does on you. For instance, if you fantasize about being raped by five muscular Tartars in a Tashkent tent, he may feel overly jealous and upset, just as *you* might if he told you that he had dreams of seducing ten 15-year-old blondes in the back seat of a white stretch Cadillac.

There are some fantasies you can share and some fantasies you can use to excite both yourself and your partner. But sexual arousal, particularly when it reaches a very high pitch, is very much a matter of individual quirks and tastes. Although I am not recommending that you conceal anything from your partner or that you hold anything back, I *am* recommending that you think for a moment before you tell him about that fantasy of being whipped by Sean Connery or sinking your teeth into Richard Gere's left buttock. You may deflate the moment of eroticism rather than heighten it. And the aim, after all, is to drive your man very wild in bed.

Sexual fantasies take numerous different forms, and everybody's fantasies are different. They don't necessarily present a true picture of your sexual personality, since many of the acts about which you find yourself fantasizing are certainly not acts in which you would really enjoy participating. Being raped or forcibly assaulted is a common sexual fantasy among women, and yet not one of the women who told me that they daydreamed of rape said that they would derive even the slightest pleasure from a real rape. The truth is quite the opposite: They would find it traumatic and degrading.

One New York woman told me that she had fantasized again and again about having intercourse with her Great Dane. She kept thinking about it, particularly when her husband was away on business trips for weeks on end. She had romped around naked with the dog and had even gone as far as masturbating it, but at the very last moment she had decided that full intercourse was something she was completely unable to contemplate. She had faced up to the fantasy and realized it was just that—a fantasy. The dog of her daydream wasn't a real dog at all, it was a feeling, an erotic invention.

If she had told her husband about her fantasy, his reaction would almost certainly have been one of shock and disgust. She still thought about the dog from time to time when she and her husband were making love, but once she had come to terms with the fantasy, she used it unashamedly to arouse herself and thus respond more avidly to her husband's lovemaking, but, of course, without sharing the idiosyncratic details, which would only have put him off. That is what you can do when you have a fantasy that you think might be "over the top" as far as your man of the moment is concerned.

On the other hand, there are plenty of times when a fantasy shared is a fantasy whose erotic power is doubled. Louise, 22, from St. Louis, Missouri, had a recurrent fantasy about being a slave girl. She told me, "I think the fantasy was originally sparked off in my mind when I was about 11 years old. We had an encyclopedia at home which showed a Roman slave girl chained to a post, with her breasts bare, and I used to take that encyclopedia under the dining room table and stare at the picture for hours on end, sometimes squeezing my legs together while I looked at it. It was the first picture that ever had any kind of sexual effect on me, and when I went to bed at night I was always fantasizing about it. Sometimes I would take off my pajamas and lie there in bed and pretend that I was this naked slave girl, and that Roman soldiers were coming around to mock me.

"I forgot about the fantasy for a long time, but as I grew older and started going out with boys, it began to come back to me. One day I told my boyfriend Ken about it while he and I were making love, and it really turned him on, especially since I'd elaborated on it since I was younger. I told him that I could imagine being his slave, all chained up, and that he would have the right to have sex with me whenever he wanted, no matter how much I protested. He could kiss me all over, and touch me, and put his fingers up me, whatever he wanted to do.

"I held onto the rails at the head of the bed, as if I were chained up, and we almost acted it out. He sat astride me, and pressed his stiff cock against my face, kind of massaging me with it. He even twisted my hair around it, and rubbed his balls against my mouth and my eyes. Then he worked his way down a bit, and squeezed his cock in between my breasts. I lifted my head up, and licked the top of his cock with the tip of my tongue, but I couldn't reach any further because I was still pretending that I was chained up. I didn't need to be chained up for real; the important thing was that we were playing out the fantasy, so it was enough to imagine it.

"Ken did everthing to me. He opened up my legs, and he slid his fingers right up inside me and massaged the inside of my cunt until it was so slippery that his hands were smothered in juice. Then he turned me around and sat on top of me with his back to me and licked my cunt and my ass until I was panting out loud with the feeling of it and aching to close my legs because that's the way I really work up toward a climax. I squeeze my legs tight together and that helps to bring me off. But Ken wouldn't allow me to close my legs. He just kept flicking and flicking at my clitoris until it felt as if it were going to explode or something and I still couldn't quite manage a climax.

"But then he turned around again, and I looked down and he was holding his cock in his fist, and he gave it three slow beats with his fist, and his white sperm sprayed all over my pubic hair. I had a climax then like no other climax I've ever had before or since. It shook me, physically shook me, while I was lying there on the bed, and still I didn't let go of the rails of the bedhead, I just clutched on to them and shook and shook.

"We play variations of the slave game every now and then. Not too often. Most of the time you want your fantasy to stay in your mind. I mean I have several versions of the same fantasy; there's quite a mild one where I'm just manacled and chained around my ankles, and I have to serve all these men with wine and food but I'm completely naked so they can touch me whenever I bend over, slipping their thumbs up my cunt and things like that. And then there's a very strong fantasy that I don't usually talk about with anyone, but it has to do with whipping, you know, with being whipped, and having all this blood running down me, but I've never discussed it with anyone, not even with Ken. I don't want him to think that I'm weird or something. But in the fantasy I've been whipped, and I'm kneeling on the floor chained up, and all these brutish kind of men come around and start urinating on me, so that all my wounds sting like hell."

It took me a long time to get Louise to tell me about her fantasy. It was only when she was convinced that thousands of other women have fantasies that seem to them just as extreme and just as shameful that she agreed to talk about it at all. She went on later to describe her fantasy in the most graphic terms. When she was very highly aroused, she could picture every detail of it in her mind's eye, the chains, the room in which she was imprisoned, the cold and the darkness, the faces of the men who were brutalizing her. She could imagine the urine mingling with the blood; she could imagine urinating herself in stimulated fright. She could imagine both the fear and the excitement as clearly as if she were actually experiencing it.

The fantasy rarely lasted more than a few seconds, a vivid glimpse at the very peak of arousal, and as soon as Louise had successfully climaxed, the fantasy would fade. It perplexed her because apart from the pretended games of being a slave that she would occasionally play with her boyfriend, which involved no pain and no blood and no actual bondage, she said that she would never consider acting out her sexual fantasy for real. The fantasy made her feel embarrassed, too, and even ("well, I have to say it,") *perverted*.

Later on, we're going to take a look at some of the things that people do to stimulate themselves and their sex partners to very high levels of erotic sensation. They include bondage of various kinds, sexual power games, masquerades, and every conceivable variety of what used to be popularly thought of as perversions. But to my mind, and to the minds of most sex counselors who have to deal with the day-to-day questions that sensible people ask about sex, bondage, urination, and dressing up in rubber are done simply to add stimulus to a happy sexual relationship and can scarcely be classed as perversions. Nobody who acts out fantasies should feel guilty or ashamed. They also should not feel ashamed even if they do nothing but fantasize.

It is perfectly normal and perfectly healthy to think so-called dirty thoughts. It simply shows that you are a full-blooded, well-adjusted woman whose sex drive is in perfect working order and whose natural curiosity about erotic subjects is in no way blunted.

Many advisers and sexologists will have tried to tell you that already. But what they may not have told you is that you can use your "dirty" thoughts to add spice and interest to your sex life and to arouse your man into thinking twice about turning over and falling asleep.

As a young New York actress explained to me, "I have two or three really strong erotic fantasies which I play out in my mind while I'm making love. Sometimes I play out part of my fantasies for real, and it's amazing how exciting they can be, like **doing something you've always dreamed of.**"

Margaret, 29, a media saleswoman from Baltimore, said, "My husband and I are both very career oriented. Dave works down at the TV station; I work up here at the ad agency. We're always having dinnners with clients, both of us, and sometimes we both arrive home about eleven o'clock, bushed, and all we can do is drink a large glass of cold white wine together and stare at each other and look forward to the weekend. But it did get to the point where we were never making love. We were always asleep or working. We got into bed and turned our backs on each other and that was it. Bed was a place to sleep, not a marital playground, like everybody kept telling us it ought to be.

"Anyway, one day I saw these two construction workers digging up the street, and they whistled at me. I glanced back and they were very good looking; very sweaty, very dirty, bare chests and muscles and chins like Mount Rushmore. I had a fantasy about them following me and dragging me down to their little hut and then lifting up my skirt and taking down my panties and fucking me, one after the other, in this little hut, which (in my fantasy, in any case) smelled of sweat and soil and tobacco. And all the walls were covered with very lewd pinups of girls with enormous breasts and their vaginas wide open.

"I had that fantasy while I was walking along the street, and when I went back to the office and started being very efficient and making appointments for the day, I suddenly realized that my panties were wet. I went to the bathroom and took them down and touched myself, and I was soaking, as if I were ready to make love. It disturbed me. I suddenly thought: I'm frustrated. I have deep sexual needs, and I'm allowing my days and my nights to slip away without any sexual satisfaction.

"I thought about it all afternoon. Then, when I

went home that night, I sat down on the floor next to Dave and I began to tell him about these two construction workers. I think he was annoyed at first. Jealous, or irritable, but I went on and I told him about the whole fantasy, about being raped in the hut and everything. Well, he didn't say a word; but he laid me down on the rug, and he kissed me, and then he slipped his hand inside my blouse, and loosened my bra, and started playing with my nipples until they were popping. He kept asking me to tell him more, what it was like inside the hut, what the construction workers smelled like, what the pictures on the wall were like.

"All the time Dave was undressing me, and then at last he slipped his hand inside my panties and started massaging my clitoris, teasing it and tweaking it, and slipping his fingers up inside me. I kept on talking more and more dirty, describing how the construction workers were all grimy and unshaven, with tattoos on their arms, and their breath stank of beer, and when they stripped off their clothes their bodies were all shiny with sweat but very muscular. One of them had a tattoo of a woman's face all around his penis. His pubic hair was all shaved off, and there on his belly was this beautiful woman's face, in blue and pink, and she was stretching open her mouth, with really luscious red lips, so that it looked as if his penis was rising out of her mouth.

"I mean, all this was complete invention, but I could see it in my mind's eye just as vividly as if it were real; this worker's thick penis pushing its way in between my legs, with this tattooed woman's face around it staring straight at my open vagina. And Dave really got into the spirit of the fantasy, he tugged off my panties and stripped off his clothes and started to make love to me, really forcibly, ramming himself up inside me, and swearing too, telling me what a fucking terrific fuck I was, things like that. Well, we went so wild it isn't easy to talk about it now without feeling kind of embarrassed. But we really let go. We ended up making love almost all night, and we both went to work the following day absolutely exhausted. But both of us had this really incredible feeling of satisfaction, this really dirty smug feeling, just like you have when you very first sleep with somebody, and you're *sure* that it shows all over your face.

"Later on, Dave began to tell me about some of his fantasies, too. I must admit that once or twice they made me jealous, or even a little inadequate. All the girls in his fantasies seemed to have such enormous breasts and I'm not particularly well-endowed. But he had one beautiful fantasy about meeting a girl at a railroad station in the Midwest somewhere, on a summer's day, with miles of wheatfields all around, and how this girl stood on the opposite side of the track and lifted up this elegant white dress she was wearing and revealed that she wasn't wearing any panties.

"Well, I actually recreated that fantasy for him when we went to New York recently to see the way they'd remodeled the Museum of Modern Art. We were looking around one of the galleries, and I stepped through to the next gallery, and lifted my dress, so that only Dave could see me through the doorway. I was wearing white pantyhose, but no panties, so Dave could see me quite clearly. I think that turned out to be the fastest tour of the Museum of Modern Art in history: Dave couldn't wait to get back to the Sheraton and make love."

You can see from Margaret's story that it can be just as arousing for you to discover what your man's sexual fantasies are as it is for him to discover what *yours* are. Most people have a key sexual fantasy, an enduring and reliable erotic image that can stimulate them almost at any time, and it would be helpful for you to find out what your man's key sexual fantasy is. As I have said before, however, this may not necessarily be an accurate reflection of his sexual personality. Some men and women have sexual fantasies that deeply disturb them, that make them feel guilty and embarrassed, and because the fantasy arouses them so much, they begin to believe that there must be something psychologically wrong with them. But those sexual daydreams that turn us on the most are not necessarily an expression of what we would really like to do.

Perhaps one of the clearest illustrations of how this works in the human mind is summed up by 26-year-old Greta, who told me, "I wouldn't mind being raped by fourteen men, provided they were all my husband." Far from being anticipatory wishes, as many of the stuffier school of psychiatry believe that they are, to me fantasies clearly seem to be a way in which the human mind can enjoy the thrill and the arousal of perverse sexual deeds without risking any of the physical or psychological trauma that might accompany them if practiced in reality.

We fantasize about being rich, about driving racing cars, about jumping out of airplanes with a parachute. These are all ways of enjoying extreme cerebral stimuli without taking the risks. Why should it be so wrong to fantasize about extreme sexual stimulation in just the same way?

Although it is probably advisable for you to keep your most wayward fantasies to yourself, do not hesitate to find out what it is that really arouses your man the most. All you have to do is to remember not to be shocked, no matter what he tells you. Some totally well-balanced men have fantasies of whipping and raping women and even of having sex with very young children. Because they have fantasies about any of these variations, that doesn't mean for a moment that they're ever likely to commit any of the sexual acts that stimulate them. It's all in the mind, and most people are strong enough and well-contained enough to keep their fantasies where they belong, inside of their heads.

The fantasies of most men, however, tend not to be sadistic but masochistic. That is, they fantasize about being dominated by some tall, self-possessed woman who is going to relieve them of any sexual responsibility.

Here are five different popular male fantasies, including how they had an effect on the couples who shared them:

1 Leonard and Sara.   Leonard came out one day and told me that he had fantasized for years and years about us taking seperate trains out to Connecticut someplace and arranging to meet as if by chance. Then we'd go into the woods and take all of our clothes off and make love without saying a word. After that we'd take seperate trains back to the city and pretend that it had never happened, that each of us had had an affair with somebody different. In the end we did it. It was a summer day, but it poured with rain. All the same, we went into the woods out near the Silvermine Tavern and we took all of our clothes off and made love in the leaves. It was strange, very erotic, but very romantic. But we didn't go back to the city by separate trains, we stayed together. We wandered for hours naked in the woods, in the rain, feeling each other, touching each other, making love two or three times. I don't quite know what it was that Leonard had been searching for in his fantasy, but it made both of us realize that we were strangers who could have a more exciting and more satisfying time together if we got to know each other a little better."

2 George and Diana.   "We were fooling

around in bed one Saturday afternoon and I said to George, 'What would you really like me to do to you to turn you on'? And he thought about it for a while and at last came out and said, 'I'd like you to spank my backside with your hairbrush.' I thought he was kidding at first, but when I laughed he got quite upset, and I realized that he wasn't kidding at all. About a week later, we went to a dinner party and both of us had too much to drink, and when we got home we were arguing like crazy. In the end, George said he was sorry, but I was still angry. 'You're always saying you're sorry,' that's what I told him. And there he was in the bathroom, naked, brushing his teeth, and I took hold of my belt and I whipped him across his bare backside. It made a vivid red mark from one side to the other; but he didn't say anything, just lowered his head. I whipped him again, and then again, and then again, criss-cross marks. I was screaming at him, 'You want to be whipped and spanked; well, here you are then!' But in the end he turned around and I was amazed to see he had a terrific erection. I held him close, and hugged him, and said I was sorry for whipping him, and all the time I gently stroked his cock up and down. It was so swollen; it was enormous. We went into the bedroom; we didn't even make it to the bed. I lay down on the floor and said, 'Quick, quick, fuck me,' and I even put my hands down between my legs and opened myself up for him with my fingers. We made love violently, and very quickly; and both of us had very strong climaxes. We made love again two or three times that night, although of course we don't do that every night. But it did change our sex lives, there isn't any doubt about that. It gave me a new feeling of sexual power, that I could do something to George to turn him on. I didn't lose any respect for him. But it made me think that I'd discovered something forbidden and thrilling, and that made *me* feel excited, too."

3 Hugh and Jane. "I was very innocent when I married Hugh. My mother had told me very little about sex, except the basic facts of reproduction. I knew as much about sex as I did about the life-cycle of the Anopheles mosquito. I'd had fantasies myself, but I didn't really know anything about sexual peculiarities or perversions. So when Hugh mentioned to me one day that—well, that he'd like to see me wearing stockings and a garter belt and high-heeled shoes to bed, you can imagine that I was pretty confused. In fact I was upset. I thought only whores wore things like that. I worried about it for days. Fortunately I had a neighbor who was very much more knowledgeable and broadminded than I was, and when I told her what Hugh had suggested, she was incredibly reassuring. She said that it had nothing at all to do with Hugh getting bored with me. She said it was something that appealed to him, that's all, and that it was a way of spicing our marriage up a little bit. We went out together and she helped me to buy some white stockings and a white garter belt. I even bought a quarter-cup bra and a pair of open panties.

"That evening, when Hugh was sitting up in bed reading, I made my entrance out of the bathroom looking like the slinkiest hooker ever. I felt nervous, but you should have seen the expression on his face. He was stunned, and surprised, but he was very excited, too. He kissed me all over, and I mean all over, my lips, my breasts, my back, my stomach, my thighs; and when he opened the white lacy slit of my panties and saw the way my pussy was bulging out of them, all pink and juicy, well, he just groaned, and I mean actually groaned. He made love to me all evening, and we ended up doggie fashion, with me on my hands and knees, and Hugh behind me, and I was furiously masturbating myself while he was fucking me, I didn't care at all, I just wanted to have a climax at the same time as his. My panties were absolutely drenched, and Hugh was clutching and squeezing my breasts, he just loved the way they stood up in that bra, it made them look so much bigger and higher.

"I think I lost all of my sexual inhibitions that night, and I'm pleased. I'll do anything now, whatever Hugh happens to feel like. I get too much pleasure out of it to feel embarrassed or ashamed. I can use explicit words now without thinking that I'm dirty or wrong. I can talk about sex quite openly. Maybe I should have been through all of this during my adolescence; but just because I didn't, that doesn't mean that I'm going to allow the fun of it to pass me by now."

4 Frank and Tina. "Frank had always had an erotic fantasy about people watching us while we made love. When we were having sex, he would say things like, 'Imagine there are people sitting around watching us do this; as if we're in a sex show; and they're really staring close to see everything we're doing, and getting turned on.' I had to admit that the idea of it turned me on as well. I've always had a secret fantasy about being a stripper, you know? When I was about fifteen or sixteen I used to perform striptease dances in front of the mirror in my bedroom and pretend that hundreds of men were watching me. Anyway, Frank had an incredible idea. He rented a video camera, and invited a whole lot of our friends around for a party, including our next-door neighbors, and then he asked them one after another to look into the camera and pretend that they were looking at a really sexy movie. None of them guessed what he was doing it for. I think they all thought that it was just a party game, because he played the video back to them, and everybody had a good laugh about it.

"But later on we took the tape to our bedroom, and played it while we made love, so that it looked as if all the people we knew, even our next-door neighbors, were watching us. It was strange at first, but Frank found it really erotic, and he made love to me in a very slow, graceful, dreamlike way. I had a climax without realizing it was going to happen. The sensation was fantastic. Usually my climaxes are very brief, but this climax went on and on forever, and every time I looked toward the television I had the feeling that these people were actually watching me having an orgasm. Neither of us would go to an orgy, at least I don't think that we would. But we might make love someplace out in the open where people might be able to see us, I don't know."

5 Jerry and Peta.   "I had already been through two broken affairs and a very short and messy marriage when I met Jerry. I had two feelings: One was that I knew everything about men and sex, and the other was that I had no desire to pander to whatever it was a man wanted. My husband behaved like a pig. No sensitivity, no romance, nothing. But Jerry struck me as different. I met him at a barbecue. He seemed quiet, almost introverted, but he had a good sense of humor, and we got on well together right from the start. After going out together for two or three weeks, we slept together, and he was extremely creative and gentle. After Tad—he was my husband—Jerry seemed like Adonis. Then once day we were walking along the beach, and Jerry said, 'Do you know, I've always wondered what people find sexy in rubber.' I was completely taken aback. I said, 'Rubber? What do you mean?' But I realized by the way in which he asked me that he'd been trying to pluck up the courage to say it to me for quite a long time. I thought to

myself: Be flattered, not frightened. If he feels he
can trust you enough to tell you his most peculiar
fantasy, then he must think quite a lot of you.

"I let him tell me about his fantasy. In fact, I encouraged him. And in the end he told me that he
had always fantasized about girls dressed up in rubber, with rubber masks on and rubber suits and
rubber boots. I have to tell you here and now that I
didn't understand it at all, and although I tried to be
calm about it, it did disturb me. I thought, Oh, God,
at last I meet a nice guy and he turns out to be some
kind of sexual freak. I felt terrible about it. I went
home and drank about a half bottle of Chivas Regal
and cried a lot.

"But the next day I realized that I was going to
have to face up to it, and it wasn't *that* terrible, even
if Jerry actually wanted me to dress up in rubber.
We met for lunch, and after a while I managed to
pluck up the courage to broach the subject again. I
said if he really wanted me to try dressing up in rubber, then I'd do it. But all he did was kiss me, and
squeeze my hand, and laugh. He said it was only a
fantasy, that was all. He didn't want me to do it;
in fact he'd never done it himself, and never at-
tempted to ask any woman to do it. As long as I understood what was going on in his head, if I didn't
mind if he talked about it when we made love. And
do you know something, that was a step forward for
me in the way I thought about men. They have a different way of fantasizing from women. They're
more . . . I don't know, *mechanical.* But that's the
way they are. And I think if a woman can understand that without being disgusted or put off, then
she's going to find that she's taken a giant leap forward in her sexual relationships."

Peta came up with a clear and very specific insight into male sexual fantasy. This kind of insight
is the key that makes it possible for a woman to un-

lock her reservations and to give her man the time of his life in bed, awarding herself at the same time all the benefits of his excitement and gratified response. Your man will probably never tell you the very deepest and most perverse fantasies that go through his head; and there is no particular need for you to know them. They are fleeting, challenging, outrageous images that he uses to achieve that last ounce of erotic stimulus just as he is about to ejaculate inside you, that last moment when nothing matters except you and him, not morals, not manners, not the world outside. And however shocking or bizarre they might seem if you were to hear them described to you on a wet Thursday afternoon, they are quite usual and acceptable in those moments when he is doing his best to achieve satisfaction not only for himself but for you, too.

All you have to do is to understand that men are psychologically different from you in many ways. They derive sexual excitement from graphic images rather than emotional moods. They are very *visual* in their approach to sex. You only have to look at a copy of *Hustler* or any of the raunchier men's magazines to see what fantastic requirements their editors are catering to: women with their legs spread wide apart, exposing their vaginas in needle sharp detail in front of the camera, often with their faces out of focus.

This has nothing to do with male chauvinism or men regarding women as sex objects, and more and more intelligent and free-thinking women are beginning to understand this. The way men respond to pinups is simply part of their automatic psychological and physiological reaction to pretty faces, bare breasts, and flaunted vaginas. Men can't help it. They find women arousing to look at. And if women could only stop thinking about this response as being degrading to their sex and instead perceive it as nothing more than a complimentary and natural reaction, then many more sexual relationships could work very much better.

Before we close the file on fantasy (and, actually, it's a whole library in itself) I want to quote a number of advertisements for hard-core pornography magazines and videos, all of which cater to male sexual fantasies. After each quotation, I want you to mark yourself 10 if you were aroused by the advertisement; 8 if you were not particularly aroused but curious to see what the product was like; 6 if you were not curious to see the product but not offended by it; 4 if you were indifferent to the advertisement and would have preferred not to have read it; 2 if you are hostile to what you have read; and 0 if you would never consider dating a man who was interested in products like these.

1. _Private_ magazine: "Full from cover to cover with gorgeous girls being fucked. A randy nun meets two fellows; and then there is a Swedish girl called Britt who enjoys being fucked and having her man come in her mouth."

2. "Tabu" video: "Four girls decide to open a brothel, 50 cents for a suck and a dollar for a fuck—see the results for yourself. A flaming family threesome and two beauties perform some slick stunts with their cunts and turn their spouses inside out."

3. "Tropic of Desire" video: "The story of the Pink Flamingo, the legendary World War II brothel in Hawaii. Sex-starved servicemen flocked there to spend a few lust-filled moments in the arms of America's most talented pleasure girls. Lots and lots of heavy rampant sex action from six lovely actresses."

4. _Girls Who Crave Big Cocks_ magazine: "Full color 100 pages of the biggest hardest cocks you have ever seen. Super huge monster cocks stuffed into tight juicy cunts, sliding in and out of wet willing lips, exploding gallons of come over mouths, tits, and faces."

5. Sex Bizarre magazine: "For the real connoisseur of golden showers or pissing. As the cover shows, there is a guy pissing all over two girls' faces. Then here is a girl who pisses all over a man's face."

6. "Final Test" video: "This film is a truly amazing one-hour cock-stretching ball-bursting porno epic. Never mind the story, just listen to what's in it—for a start the biggest clit I've ever seen—this girl has a clit almost like a miniature cock. Bondage, whipping, male and female domination, an incredible lesbian scene where two girls fill each other's cunts with water and then piss it out. Really way out video with lots of juicy sticky come shots."

You may never have seen any pornography. You may never have wanted to. But all of the above quotations are from genuine advertisements (you can probably tell how authentic they are by the panting way in which they are written), and all of them are specifically aimed to excite archetypal male sexual fantasies. Part of the reason I have quoted the advertisements is to shock you—to make you realize that inside of your man's mind there is an anything-goes world of extraordinary sex. Another, more practical, reason is to help you judge your reaction to them and to broaden your outlook on the diverse and sometimes disturbing world of sexual stimulation.

The advertisements—and the products they advertise—are blatant and explicit. There are entire magazines and films devoted to bondage and transsexualism. There is even a magazine called *New Cunts*: a lavish full-color production that guarantees its readers that every model has her pubic hair shaved off. There is a monthly magazine called

Anal Sex that shows nothing else but girls being penetrated anally, and sometimes vaginally at the same time. Anything and everything you can imagine and many things that you will *never* imagine are depicted in magazines, on film, and on video.

Personally, I believe it is very important for every woman who wants to understand and satisfy her man to confront the strongest realities of the male sexual imagination. Although you are psychologically far less responsive to pornography than your partner, taking a look at a selection of porno magazines and videos will give you an inside view of what form his fantasies may be taking. Ask him to view them with you, ask him what turns him on and what doesn't. He may be shy at first to admit that he finds them arousing, but by the end of the evening you may very well discover that you know more about his sexual tastes than ever before. You may also discover that you know more about *your* sexual tastes than ever before.

As our five examples of male sexual fantasies showed, most of them remained wholly or partially in the imagination of the man concerned, even when he shared them with his partner. Jerry didn't actually want Peta to dress up in rubber wear; Frank was content with a video of people watching them rather than a real audience; and once Leonard had made love to Sara in the woods, he was quite content to return home with his fantasy unfinished.

Fantasies are not an expression of sexual obsession or perversion or "dirtiness." When your man fantasizes about making love to other women, he is not betraying you in any way, any more than you are betraying him when you fantasize about making love to other men. Fantasies are an indication of the strength of your sexual imagination, and that is all. As such they should not only be respected, but discussed freely and incorporated whenever practicable and desirable into your active sex life.

Some fantasies, as we have seen, are best kept inside your own head. You know your man. You can be the best judge of which fantasies, once revealed, may put him off. But if you *do* tell him one of your deeper fantasies and it *does* throw him off-balance and upset him, make it clear that you expect as much understanding from him as he would get from you if he were to tell you some of his most private turn-ons. And if he's still huffy—show him this chapter. That should put some sense into him.

I have dealt with the potent subject of fantasy quite early on in this book. First, because I think imagination is crucial to really good sex. Second, because I want you to be as deeply shocked now as you're ever going to be (if you're *not* shocked, but simply hungry for more, you're doing very well).

In a while we're going to be talking about some of the more extreme things that you can do to drive your man wild in bed, some of the fantasies that you might consider bringing to life; and for that you need a rather unshockable attitude.

The good thing to remember about sex is that it is for pleasure and emotional communication only (apart from reproduction), and that neither partner should ever try to impose anything on the other that doesn't bring about mutual enjoyment and satisfaction. If you find you're involved in something you don't really like, then you have *the absolute and indisputable right* to say no, I don't like this.

Now, let's take a look at what he expects you to be—his fantasy, in effect, of the perfect woman and how far you can and should fulfill that fantasy.

9

Can You Be the Woman He Wants?

"I want a friend, I want a wife, I want a lover, I want a whore, I want a princess, I want a critic, I want a business partner, I want a hostess, I want a mother for my children; I want someone who makes me laugh, someone who understands me when I'm down, someone who forgives me when I'm unjust, and stands up to me when I'm angry. I want someone who can walk into a room beside me and make me feel like I'm royalty. I want someone who can talk dirty and really turn me on. I want someone whose lips can speak words of warmth, words of reason, and words of judgment, yet will use those same lips to kiss my penis."

These are the requirements of over thirty men to whom I talked for the purposes of preparing this chapter. I simply asked them what kind of woman they really wanted, and that, in sum, was the answer.

Perhaps the most extraordinary thing about the female personality, and especially about the female personality that is emerging from the new social freedoms of today, is that it is capable of fulfilling almost all of these varied and sometimes contradictory desires. Women have remarkable resilience and flexibility, born not of being subservient or inferior to men, but of the deep and far-reaching demands that nature has always made on them.

Psychologically, men are far less flexible in their behavior, since they are not required to change so radically and so abruptly during the course of a single day. Even full-time career women do not carry working attitudes back into their homes and their social life as much as men do. "Once I quit that desk in the evening, that's it, I become feminine and pretty and light. I've been making decisions all day, telling everybody what to do. I want to be told what to do by somebody else. Perferably handsome, and smelling of Chanel aftershave."

We have already seen that in first encounters and at times when a sexual relationship may be flagging, men do secretly prefer you to come on strong. But how do they want you to act during a long-term sexual relationship? For the past ten years, the social pattern throughout the United States has been altering very much more in favor of the long-term rather than the short-term sexual relationship—assisted not so much by fear of venereal diseases, but by the growing up and maturing of those who originally engendered the Permissive Society of the 1960's. Those sexual freedoms in which the permissive generation reveled so self-indulgently have now been accepted and established and are no longer novel, so the generation that has come after them feels no need to seek the same erotic thrills. They have learned, too, that longer relationships tend to be more satisfying, more pleasurable, and ultimately more exciting.

"I used to date dozens of boys when I was eighteen and nineteen, and I used to sleep with almost all of them. I couldn't tell you how many boys I've slept with. It all seemed so outrageous at the time. I think part of the thrill was knowing that my parents would be utterly scandalized if they knew. Now that I'm living with Larry, I regret every one of those boys. The sex meant nothing. I didn't even learn anything. The kind of sexual experiences that Larry and I are having today make those one-night stands seem like diddling.''

There can be no hard-and-fast definitions of what a man wants from a woman during a long-term relationship. As the opening to this chapter has clearly illustrated, most men seem to expect women to be fifteen different personalities at once; whereas when I put the same question to women about men, the responses were much more practical. "I want a man who knows what he wants, somebody determined." "I want somebody sophisticated and suave." "I like men to be athletic, keyed up." Whereas men are seeking multiple personalities, women are seeking complete individuals with particular characteristics.

This is not to say that there is anything wrong in that men are looking for when they enter into a long-term relationship with you. Like most women, you are capable both physically and mentally of being a cook and bottle washer one minute and a seductive siren the next. Whether you *want* to take on those roles or not is a different matter.

Just because you have approached this book with the idea of driving your man wild in bed, just because you are prepared to be more positive and more go getting in your sex life, just because you have accepted that in order to please your man there are certain sexual acts that you must consider trying and certain sexual attitudes that you must consider adopting, none of this means that you have to surrender any of your feminine independence. In fact, it is my strong belief that the more positive and expressive a woman like you allows herself to be, the more sexually attractive you will eventually be to the man in your life. Men who treat women superciliously or discourteously are nothing more or less than afraid of you; afraid of your strength, afraid of your abilities, afraid of your wide emotional and social range. They are afraid, too, of your sexuality; afraid of that one moment when they have to show you their virility and prove that they can satisfy you. That is why you have no reason at all to be anxious about men who behave like male chauvinist pigs (MCPS). They are revealing by their very chauvinism that they already secretly believe you have the upper hand, both emotionally and sexually.

An intelligent and sympathetic man will be delighted if you make the effort to become more positive in your approach not only to sex but to life in general. An MCP may be less pleased. He may go out of his way to bait you and to humiliate you, but in a moment we'll see how to deal with him and make him a happier person, too. Remember: He's only doing it because he feels threatened. If he's not doing it because he feels threatened, then believe me, he isn't worth knowing. He's what you might accurately call emotional trash.

To give your long-term relationship with the man you love that continuous golden glow of affection and eroticism, more than anything else learn to speak your mind. Never be afraid to tell your lover what you think or what you fantasize about (with those exceptions that we mentioned in the previous chapter). Always make him feel that you trust him, that you are willing to confide your emotional and sexual thoughts in him, and that he, in turn, can confide his emotional and sexual thoughts in you.

Ask his opinion about the way you look, the clothes you wear, the things you want to do. And ask his opinion, too, about the way you make love to

him. Not, perhaps, at the actual moment of your orgasm, but the following day, in the evening, when
you're thinking about bed and all the pleasures that
could be in store for you. Ask him if he likes the way
you do this or that or if there's anything he'd particularly like you to do. He may be shy. He may be un-
used to such intimate questioning and feel afraid to
hurt your feelings, in which case he'll tell you that
you're absolutely terrific in bed and that there
isn't a single thing that he can think of that would
improve your technique. He's lying, of course. But
take his lie in the best possible way, and make sure
that you bring the subject up again later.

Make sure that you know his tastes in food,
clothes, art, music, movies, books, TV, pizza, sport,
and sex. *Explore* him; you're going to be spending a
whole lot of time with him and you're going to be
sharing the most intimately communicative act
with him that two human beings can ever share.

In return, tell him about yourself, what you like,
what you don't like, what frightens you, what
arouses you. Tell him who you are. I've met so may
victims of broken marriages and fractured relationships who suddenly realize when it's far too late
that they've been spending ten years of their lives
with somebody they didn't know at all. I did it myself, so I know just how it can happen. I'm not sure if
she even told me what her name was.

Explore each other physically, the way that I've
suggested in the earlier chapters in this book. Get to
know his penis and his testicles, so that you can
handle them with confidence and friendly familiarity. Open his zipper when he's sitting watching television, and simply play with him. Find out what
kind of rubbing he prefers, whether he likes to be
tickled lightly or masturbated firmly. Do it in bed,
when he's asleep; see if you can't wake him up.
Hold him, run your hands over his whole body. Not

only on those occasions when you feel like making love, but when you don't. You'd be surprised how much more frequently you do.

All this kind of behavior is forward, go getting, and independent. But it's very arousing, too. And if you keep it up, if you *always* treat your man as somebody you want to touch and want to explore, then the rewards you will reap will be beyond measure.

To begin with, you will have to make a considerable effort to overcome your own reticence and his. He may be irritated, even shocked, if you slip your hand inside his pants and start masturbating him while he's painting the living room wall. But don't let him put you off. Show that you're demanding, that you need sex as much as he does, and that you're prepared to be positive to get it. If he tells you that you're sex mad, agree with him.

Only one point of caution here: If he's genuinely tired, if he really doesn't feel like playing the game, even after your very best tickling and teasing, then don't do what so many *men* do, don't sulk and pout and make out that you're desperately upset, and that it's every woman's right to have sex with her husband. Smile and withdraw gracefully, and show him as much affection as you can muster. And then, later, when you're lying in bed with him, hold his hand with one of your hands, and masturbate yourself with the other. Don't be shy or ashamed. Make him understand that there will always be times when one or the other of you is tired, or unable to make love because of sickness or some other reason, and tell him that if it ever happens to him, you won't worry if *he* masturbates, too—as long as he does it openly as you have. It's surprising how often tired or sick partners, once they feel their lover growing increasingly aroused, will suddenly overcome even the most overwhelming of exhaustions and want to join in. All to your benefit, of course.

In a long-term relationship, make yourself just one promise: that *every single day you will do something sexy.* It may be nothing more than kissing your man with one of those passionate, open-mouthed kisses that he always used to love so much. It may be nothing more than calling him up at work and telling him that you're aching to make love to him and that you can just imagine his hard cock sliding up inside you. It may be lovemaking. It may be dressing in something eye-catchingly sexy. Just remember to do it every day, and make it varied and unexpected. That way, you will not only drive your man wild in bed, but you will probably keep him forever.

The way you dress and undress in front of your man is of tremendous importance, not only to your sex life but to the way he feels about you all the time. I'm not talking about sexy underwear and striptease; I'm simply talking about the way you look every day, your erotic chic.

One day borrow one of his shirts and do the housework in nothing else at all. Sandra, a 27-year-old fashion-store assistant from Hollywood, tried it, and told me about it: "Rick was at home all Friday, working. I tried to get him to talk to me, but he was too busy, and there was nothing but phone call after phone call. I gave him a glass of white wine but he scarcely drank it. I don't know. I just felt like half an hour of his time. In the end, I took a shower, and washed my hair, and then instead of getting properly dressed again, I went into the bedroom and put on one of Rick's blue-checked workshirts. I did up a couple of buttons, but that was all. And I did put high-heeled sandals on, too. But then I started cleaning the kitchen, dressed like that, and I could tell that Rick had noticed me through the doorway, because he kept glancing up and frowning.

"In the end he came into the kitchen and I was washing the floor. I was bending over to scrape off some stuff from under the dishwasher. Rick knelt down behind me, and ran his finger all the way down the curve of my back, and touched my bare bottom, and tickled my pussy. I turned around, and he took me into his arms, and gave me the most fantastic kiss on the month. We made love right there and then on the kitchen floor, amongst all the warm water and the soapsuds. And in the end he picked me right up off the tiles, and was holding me right up in the air and making love to me like that. Nobody had ever done anything like that to me before. I was riding him just like a horse, and every time I came down on his cock it forced itself so deep inside of me I felt as if it were touching my heart."

You don't always have to walk around the house with no panties on, but you should always dress as if you've done it to attract him; as he, in return, should dress to attract you. A tight pair of pedal-pushers (under which you're either wearing nothing at all or a G-string); a bright smart designer T-shirt; bright beads and your hair curled—you don't need much more than that to look sexy and smart. But even a man who doesn't know anything at all about fashion or grooming will notice and resent it if your hair is dirty, or if your nails are chipped, or if you haven't even made the most minimal effort to look attractive.

Most of the time, the clothes to which men respond the most are not the sexiest ones. They are the clothes that make you suit the personality trait that most strongly attracts him toward you. If it's your sophistication that arouses him, then he will like you in classy well-tailored dresses and upscale jewelry and hats; if he sees you as innocent and fresh, then a gingham dress with puff sleeves and a Peter Pan collar may very well turn him on just as much as the deepest of décolleté necklines.

Talking of necklines, it is glaringly apparent from the way that women dress today that many of them are still uncertain about what to do with their breasts. So many women with very small breasts make an attempt to conceal what they consider to be their shortcomings by wearing dresses or blouses that button right up to the neck or by wearing large sloppy T-shirts or sweaters. The result is invariably to make them appear as if they're completely flat-chested—the opposite of what they're trying to achieve. My motto is, if you haven't got it, flaunt it. Try wearing tight T-shirts with no bra. Try wearing blouses open right down to the last possible button. Try wearing elegant dresses with low necklines and well-fitting tops. Most men are far from scathing about small breasts; a high percentage prefer them to the larger, *Playboy*-sized variety. And when you're around the house, you can go topless, wearing nothing but jeans, and if that doesn't turn him on, he's probably seriously ill, or dead.

Equally, many girls with large breasts go to remarkable lengths to hide them. They stoop when they walk to try to make them look smaller; they always wear tops over jerkins over loose sleeveless sweaters or flowing dresses. I know how embarrassed and self-conscious they often feel, how often men stare at them in unashamed lust and seem to carry on every conversation with their cleavage rather than with their face. But those girls who *have* come to terms with their bust size and who make the best of their breasts in thin-knit sweaters, deep-plunging neckline dresses, or smart designer blouses always look beautiful and desirable, not in spite of their breasts but *because* of them.

To cite an extreme example, baseball's famous "kissing bandit," Morganna, the girl who regularly jumps over the fence to plant kisses on baseball stars such as George Brett and John Candelaria, has a 60-24-39 figure and still manages to look groomed and beautiful in tight T-shirts and silky running shorts.

Dressing smartly and sexily shouldn't be one sided, either. He should dress to please you, too, and you should tell him when he doesn't. You may get some arguments of the "favorite sweater" variety, but in the end he'll appreciate you for smartening him up. A man who knows he looks good will always have more sexual confidence; and, again, you'll be the beneficiary.

Time and time again, in all areas of your relationships—from what you're wearing to how you like to have your clitoris stimulated—*communication* is the most important word of all. I can't count the number of couples I've talked to whose relationships have broken down and who always seem to have the same excuse: "I just didn't realize how he felt." "How was I to know that she wanted me to do that?"

It is essential for you as a woman to establish your identity in your relationship, to value your own contribution to it, and to make sure that your partner values it, too. This doesn't mean brow beating or haranguing him or constantly telling him that he doesn't appreciate how hard you work. But it *does* mean exciting his awareness to what you think and how you feel, and you can only do that by explaining yourself, frankly and clearly, and speaking up when you don't agree with him.

It also means having the courage to criticize him when he isn't satisfying you in bed. Now, this is always a delicate subject. As we have seen in a whole **variety of circumstances, a man's sexual pride is** very important to him and is closely connected to his performance. But the age of *pretending* that you are satisfied in bed is long gone. It went out with hula hoops and mismatched shoes and socks, or at least it should have. If your man isn't driving *you* wild in bed, then you will never be able to drive *him* wild in bed.

Kelly, 26, a secretary from Butte, Montana, went through three dissatisfied years with her husband Gerry before she found the nerve to tell him that he wasn't giving her what she wanted. But she did it in a very careful and sympathetic way, aware that she could have seriously hurt his feelings and undermined his sexual confidence.

"Gerry's a great guy, very good looking, very sincere, but when we got married I don't think he had any experience of women at all. The first few months it was okay, because we made love almost all of the time. But then he got promoted at the electrical plant where he works, and he began to get more and more tied up at the office every night. He was always tired when he got home; but even when he wasn't, he didn't make love any better. It was just a question of wash your teeth, get into bed, stick it up me, and go to sleep. I was so frustrated I was starting to have nightmares about sex, and I could hardly bear Gerry to touch me. Well, I read a book about sex, and then I went and talked to my doctor. He was very sympathetic about it, surprisingly, and told me that I had to make Gerry wake up to his shortcomings or else our marriage was going to break up, and he meant sooner rather than later.

"What I did was to make the first move. I think that's usually the problem when a man isn't making love very well; the wife just lies there and curses her ill-luck instead of doing something positive. I didn't feel particularly turned on to Gerry at that time, but I knew that I was going to have to do it if I wanted to save our relationship; and the truth was that I *did* love him, very dearly. So when he was in bed one evening, I got into bed nude, which I don't usually do, and I started to kiss him and stroke him. He said, 'Not tonight, Kelly, come on, I've got an early start tomorrow,' but I wouldn't stop. I wouldn't let him get away with it.

"I unbuttoned his pajamas and kissed his chest, and then I opened up his pants and started caressing his penis. He didn't know what to say. In fact, I don't think he would have said anything even if he *had* known what to say. But words weren't necessary. His penis rose up really hard, and I rubbed it and stroked it and then I went down the bed a little and licked it and started to make love to it with my mouth. I'm blushing a little bit now because I'd never ever done that before, and I don't think that night that I was very good at it, but I was good enough to rouse Gerry up. He stripped off his pajamas, and he tried to push me back on the bed so that he could get on top of me, but I wouldn't let him. Instead, I sat astride his chest, and ruffled my hands through his hair, and then I lifted myself up so that I was holding on the the bed rail, and I lowered my wide-open pussy right over his face.

"That was the only time I was really tense; that was the only time when I wasn't sure that it was going to work out. Because Gerry had never done anything like that to me, not lick me out, and I was terrified that he was going to say, get off, this is disgusting. I closed my eyes and waited for a moment, and then God help me I felt the tip of his tongue against my lips, licking them, and probing up into my vagina. Then he started kissing my pussy, he didn't have any idea how to do it, but they were beautiful deep kisses and I adored them. Now, he really began to turn me on, and he must have realized it, because he began to lick me faster, and suck at me, and he began to move his own body as well. Suddenly I felt something wet and warm licking at my back, and I realized what had happened. Gerry had been so aroused that he had ejaculated, and the sperm had shot all over my back. His penis began to sink away, but I was determined that I was going to be satisfied that night. I went down on him again, and very slowly started to rub him and lick him.

"Can you believe that we'd been married for three years and this was the first time I'd ever put him into my mouth, the first time I'd ever tasted his sperm? And he began to rise up again, after five or ten minutes, and soon he was just as hard as he was before. He kept telling me that he loved me, that he thought I was fantastic, and again and again he kept trying to push me onto my back, but I wouldn't let him. I thought, just for once see that a woman can take charge. I sat on top of him, and I held his erection in my hand and showed him how to get it into me, and then I went up and down on him, very slowly, not letting him push into me too far, just gripping the head of his penis with my vagina. He kept wanting to push in deeper, to do it quickly, to get it over with, but I wouldn't allow it.

"We did it slowly, really slowly, and I could feel my orgasm coming like a distant train, a dark distant train that I couldn't see, but only feel, coming nearer and nearer and nearer, and I knew that I wasn't going to resist it, that I was just going to let it come, and then it reached me, and hit me, and I have never felt anything like that orgasm in my life. It doubled me up. For a moment I thought I was dead. I wasn't even aware of Gerry at that moment, only this long dark train which was right up inside my vagina, only this shaking, and trembling, and then a feeling like colored paints, spreading and spreading in a pool."

Despite the romantic quality of her description,

Kelly's positive action in showing Gerry how to make love to her marked the beginning of a new era in their marriage; and although their sex life didn't improve overnight, it began month by month to grow more constructive, more exciting, and more satisfying.

When I discuss sexual activity with many women, I get the response, "Oh, no, I couldn't do anything like that with *my* husband . . . not with *my* lover." And it's true that, on paper, talking about sex can sometimes seem quite shocking. Most of the women I talked to had never used sexual words in front of anyone except their husbands or boyfriends; and a high proportion had never used any sexual words at all, in front of anybody.

One of the difficulties of sexual communication so often ignored by so-called comprehensive guides to sex is that many people have difficulty talking to their lovers or spouses about sex because they find it almost impossible to use language like "fuck" or "cock" or "cunt" or even "vagina" and "penis." It is the inheritance of centuries of sexual hypocrisy that we have no lyrical and acceptable words for those parts of the body that are the focus of our most intense physical feelings toward each other and no simple and graceful words for the act of deepest affection.

When talking to the women whose words appear in this book, I encouraged them to use "dirty" words for several reasons. One reason was that the "dirty" words are usually far more specific than the "clean" words. "Making love" encompasses anything from fluttering your eyelashes at a man on a park bench to complete intercourse. Another reason was that if you can learn to use words like these without too much embarrassment, you will not only be able to explain yourself more clearly to your lover, you will probably arouse him at the same time.

If you make a determined effort to liberate yourself from your own reticence about sexual words and the feeling they still convey, even today, that talking about cocks and cunts is somehow smutty, then you will find that you are able not only to excite your lover, but you are able to make it far easier for both of you to talk about the way you feel when you have sex together. And that can only lead to better sex.

The best way to get used to saying the words is to *say* them. Sit by yourself and say them out loud; then look in a mirror and say them to yourself. Pronounce them slowly and with relish. Say them in the shower while you soap yourself. Say them while you masturbate. Get used to hearing your voice pronounce them, one by one. If you can, make a tape recording of yourself being extravagantly dirty, and play it back to yourself. Does it make you blush? Do it again; you'll get used to it.

I'm not, of course, suggesting that you start to include words like these in your everyday vocabulary, because if there's one thing that makes most men cringe, even the most sophisticated and broadminded of them, it's hearing a woman swear in public. No matter how much of a whore a man likes his woman to be in bed, he always prefers her to behave like a lady in company.

Men have a strong sense of pride of ownership in the women they're dating or living with, and even though you shouldn't allow your man to be ridiculously jealous whenever you go out together (you're an independent person, you can talk to whomever you like, a man or a woman), you should appreciate that you can give him a kick by occasionally showing that you and he belong together. A little squeeze of his arm, a little kiss, a couple of affectionate words. You'd be surprised what wonders they work, and you'd also be surprised how few women ever take the trouble to think about giving them publicly to the man they love the most. Don't let some other woman do it for him; start today to do it yourself. If he asks, "What's come over you all of a sudden?" just say, "All of a sudden I remembered how much I love you." But don't forget to be just as nice to him tomorrow.

Another important part of communication in a long-term relationship is getting to know and understand his interests and his hobbies. If he's a sports freak, he can't legitimately expect you to acquaint yourself with the ins and outs of major league baseball or take an enthusiastic interest in who knocked out whom after how many rounds at Madison Square Garden. But do ask him questions about his interests, even if you find them excruciatingly boring, and do make an effort to listen to what he has to say about them. After all, he's the man you love, and if he finds something interesting in it, then maybe there is something interesting in it.

Here's Lydia, a 28-year-old music teacher from Dallas, Texas: "Dan was always a stamp freak. He'd been collecting postage stamps ever since he was a small boy, and I think his stamp albums meant more to him than almost anything. When I first lived with him, he used to drive me insane with all of these sticky little stamps all over the place, while I was supposed to sit beside him in silence and do macrame or watch 'Star Trek' or something. I really got to hate his hobby, and it became like a battleground between us. You know? It really created tensions. But one day when I was in the post office mailing some parcels, I saw a beautiful collection of new U.S. stamps. They weren't rare or special, of course. I couldn't have afforded anything like that. But they were very pretty. I bought them for him, and I packaged them up in shiny paper, and just gave them to him. He was so pleased that I'd actually thought of doing it, and I was pleased too, and he showed me how to mount them, and told me how they were made and printed and everything, and gradually I started to take an interest in what he was doing with stamps, and what they meant. I'm not a freak, and I never will be, but just making an effort to understand his hobby made all the difference, it took all the argument out of it. I guess in a way I'd been jealous of the time he spent on it, but I'd suddenly learned that there was no contest. I didn't have anything to fear from his stamp collecting as long as I didn't *make* it something to fear. Now we have a joke about it. I say, 'I'll buy you a British Guiana 1847 stamp for Christmas if you come upstairs right now and make love to me now.' I don't know whether I'll ever be able to afford the stamp, but I get all the lovemaking I want."

Make sure that you're reasonably well-read and reasonably well-informed so that you can hold a half-decent conversation on almost any topical subject. Even if you only read *Time* magazine every week and the *Reader's Digest*, that's better than nothing at all. Learn one or two funny lines or quotations, such as "What good is happiness? It doesn't buy money." Make a conscious effort to be witty and lighthearted and *fun*. It's surprising how few women remember to be amusing once they're married. Flirt with your man the way you did when you first went out together. More than anything else, show him that you don't take him for granted. Buy him a little gift, or a card, or a bunch of flowers now and again. A long-term relationship should be a constant celebration of the fact that you love each other and that you have decided to share every day together—not to mention every night.

Time and time again, I see women letting themselves down in one of the most crucial areas of their relationships, and that is the way they behave when a man takes them out to dinner. Now, it may not sound like much, it may sound picky, but knowing how to respond to a man who is wining and dining you can make all the difference between an evening of romance and an evening of resentment.

To begin with, you should remember that most men take you out to dinner to show off their style and their knowledge and their sophistication, and that it is important for you to be impressed, if indeed there is anything to be impressed about. I'm not suggesting, of course, that you applaud a complete klutz who spills soup all over your new evening dress and has an absurd argument with the waiter; but if your man is making a genuine effort to give you a good time, allow him to do so and accept his effort gracefully. I have seen so many women complaining and snarling and sulking in restaurants to the humiliation and embarrassment of their escorts that I really think it's time that somebody wrote an entire book on how a woman should behave when she's taken out to eat.

If your man is paying, he is your host. If you're going Dutch, then he is still your host. Even if *you're* paying, you should allow him the courtesy of placing the order with the waiter, of expressing any complaints or requests that either of you may have, and generally of treating you like a lady. These days, it is quite acceptable if you know more about wine than he does and for you to taste the wine; and it is quite acceptable for you to take the check openly, rather than slide the money across the table in the palm of your hand. But don't be ostentatious about it, any more than you expect *him* to be ostentatious. With independence comes self-control.

Get to know something about good food and wine, if you don't already. There is nothing more galling for a man who has taken you out to an expensive French restaurant than to hear you order steak and salad, which you could have had at Denny's. Most French restaurants these days print translations of their dishes and explain what they are; but it's still worth knowing the French words for the things that you happen to like and taking the trouble to buy a French cookbook so that you know what *Proven-çcale*, or *Mornay*, or *farci* mean. The same goes for Italian food, such as *calamare*. I remember the times that I have seen girls happily ordering fried calamare, not realizing it was squid.

You don't have to know every dish in every language. *Sag krog pu* is Thai for crab sausage, in case you've ever wondered; and *nam prik* isn't what you think it is. But do eat adventurously; do try new dishes; do allow yourself to be guided not only by your man but by the menu. Ask his advice: He wants to impress you, so give him the chance to do it.

If he is an indomitably dull eater himself, don't chide him for it. Just make your own choice and enjoy it; and maybe give him a taste of yours to liven up his palate.

When you're actually eating, eat with elegance, but never be afraid to pick up anything in your fingers if it's too tricky to eat with a knife and fork (and while you're doing it, ask him to order you a finger bowl).

Learn a little about wine, both foreign and domestic. When he's paying, you can certainly state your preference for a red or a white, a dry or a medium, but do leave the final choice up to him unless he's quite obviously floundering. Selecting the wine is one of the semimacho things that men still like to do, and I don't think that you'll be compromising your feminine independence if you accept his choice with thanks.

Wine is a very simple business these days. Don't ever allow the wine waiter to befuddle you with mystique, particularly since very few American restaurants have a wine list that is anything but straightforward and practical. If you're having a cheap, mass-produced wine with your meal, like Soave or Verdicchio or Paul Masson, all you have to do is to make sure that it's chilled to your liking; then ask the wine waiter to pour it out straight away. If you swill it around your mouth and act like a wine connoisseur, you'll only be revealing your lack of knowledge and the wine waiter will probably go back to his cellar and have a good chortle up his sleeve.

Similarly, it is a curiously ostentatious habit in American restaurants to present you with the cork when the wine is open. You can certainly check the cork to make sure that it isn't broken or crumbly, but *don't* pick it up and sniff it. You have to be a trained wine taster of many years' experience and standing to be able to tell anything meaningful from the smell of the cork.

In all, be experimental, allow yourself to be introduced to new foods and new wines, but remember that the ultimate test is whether you like them or not. If your man takes you out for a meal and you absolutely hate it, don't be afraid to say so. If it's badly cooked, ask him to complain on your behalf. If you simply can't stomach it, then tell him and give him the opportunity to order something else for you. But remember that there is nothing more upsetting for a man than for you to say, "It's all right, but I'm not hungry anymore; don't order me anything else." At least allow him to feel that he's managed to put things right for you. That's what I mean by response.

After dinner, let the romance begin. Never be afraid to be romantic; never be afraid to tell him that you love him; never be afraid to ask him to take you for a drive to see your favorite view and kiss him in the car. When I said earlier that you should do something sexy every day, I should have added "and something romantic, too." Out of romance will come confidence—confidence that he's impressed you and that he's given you an evening to remember. And out of that confidence will come more love and better loving.

I asked you at the beginning of this chapter how far you could go to become the woman of your man's dreams. The answer is *all the way*, if you're prepared to be thoughtful, appreciative, and positive, if you're prepared to remember that relationships do need to be worked at in many large and small ways. The pleasure and the amusement that you will get out of your relationship will increase with every effort you make to improve his pleasure and amusement.

Today, go out and buy him a present. Nothing expensive. Just something to show that you care. Wrap it up beautifully, and make sure that you give him a card with it that says, "I love you."

10

Making Love—How, When, and Where

The act of sexual intercourse stands way ahead of any other human activity as the most frequently practiced yet competently performed pastime. You make better love more often than you play tennis, yet I'll bet your backhand is better than your missionary position. As we have discussed before, the trouble is that because sex is almost always performed in private, without trainers or critics looking on, mistakes are perpetuated from onc act to thc next, and that it is usually only the shock of a broken relationship that makes us think: "Well, perhaps I'm not doing it as well as I could."

Ten years ago, In *How to Drive Your Man Wild in Bed*, I radically altered sexual thinking on the subject of love play by insisting, as I still insist today, that it isn't a preamble to making love but an *integral part* of it. The act of intercourse does not simply involve the insertion of the male penis into the female vagina (as stated in many handbooks) but is the careful and gradual stimulation of both partners from the first romantic embrace to the final orgasmic moment.

I am almost tempted to spread the net of my definition of sexual intercourse even wider and say that it begins when two people first meet and are attracted to each other, because it is only by seeing the stimulation of your man as a *continuous process* that your love life will expand and improve and bring you all the rewards that both your mind and your body are capable of giving you.

I am certainly going to say that the moment of orgasm should no longer be regarded as the completion of the act of intercourse but should be seen as the moment of providing physical and emotional release in an act that should continue after you have reached your climax and after he has ejaculated.

Most textbooks say that you should lie in each other's arms, exchanging words of affection and praise, and I'm certainly not going to quibble with that. I don't know of any couple who lie in each other's arms nearly often enough, exchanging words of affection and praise. But I believe that more can be done than that, that what happens after you make love should be regarded as a sharing of the feeling of sexual satisfaction, as well as a preparation for the next time. In effect, you should never stop making love all through your relationship. Even when you're apart, you should be working toward the achievement of that perfect intimacy with which sex rewards you.

I have devised (and tried) a number of simple but loving techniques that you can use to follow the act of intercourse—techniques that will reaffirm your feelings for the man you love and show him that he has satisfied you, that you appreciate what he has done for you, and that you are looking forward to more. The pleasant part about using these techniques is that more quite often comes sooner than you expect it.

Before we discuss these after-sex techniques, however, I want to talk about positions for intercourse. Because of the influence of the *Kama Sutra* and other Oriental manuals of sex, many women still believe that fancy sex equals fancy positions. There are several books that you can buy that show couples in any number of extraordinary positions, many of which seem to involve sitting on a kitchen chair. I was once asked to write the text for one of these books, and I had in all honesty to point out that in 70 percent of them, insertion of the penis into the vagina was virtually impossible, let alone doing any kind of thrusting movement to bring about mutual stimulation.

To me, the most important criterion when judging the effectiveness of a sexual position is *comfort.* Your sexual organs are so richly endowed with nerves that it takes very little actual physical movement to produce a pleasurable effect, so the spread eagling of your arms and legs, or the twisting up of your body, or any other contortions are only visually stimulating, if at all.

When it comes to intercourse, you will achieve a far greater degree of erotic pleasure if your body is comfortably positioned on a bed or a blanket so that you can forget everything but the sexual fantasies going on inside of your mind and those tingling vaginal nerves. There are few things worse than being right on the brink of a climax, only to be held back by the unwarranted intrusion of cramp or some other diverting sensation, such as the cutting of the kitchen chair seat into the cheeks of your bottom. But you can certainly use different and varied positions during the buildup to intercourse.

Susan, 31, talks about sex with her lover Phil: "Last year there was a very heavy thunderstorm, and when Phil came back from Cambridge he drove the car straight into the garage. I'd just taken a shower, and I was wrapped only in a towel. He came in soaking wet and I told him to take off his wet things and get himself into the tub. He said there were some papers and a bottle of wine in the car, and would I get them for him. So I went into the garage, and opened up the car, but there were so many papers strewn across the back seat, I didn't know which ones he wanted. I called out, 'Phil!' and he came into the garage, rubbing himself dry, as naked as I was. He took hold of me and gave me a kiss, and I kissed him back; and the next thing I knew, he had let his towel drop, and he was standing there in the garage with a big stiff cock. He kissed me some more, and I massaged his cock with my hand, then he gently tugged my towel off and began to run his hands all over my body. He turned me around so that I had my back to him, and I think at first he was thinking of fucking me like that, standing up from behind, but it was too difficult.

"So what he did was kiss me all the way down my spine, slowly kneeling down, and then he parted the cheeks of my bottom and started to push his tongue into my anus. I was pressed against the wet car, completely naked. Phil gently parted my thighs with his hands, and began to lick all around my anus and then all around my cunt, tugging at my pubic hair with his teeth, and then slipping his tongue right up inside me. Then he stood up, and picked me up, and laid me right across the hood of the car, on my back, with my legs wide apart; and he bent his head forward and he gave me the most incredible licking of my whole life, flicking my clitoris and then pressing his whole face into my cunt, and rubbing it backwards and forwards so that his cheeks were smothered in love juice. I was spread eagled over the car, and my skin was squeaking against the wet metal; stark naked in the garage in the middle of the night, with the rain beating on the roof. Phil slowly worked his finger up my anus, licking me very quickly at the same time, but really gently, scarcely touching my clitoris; he worked his finger right up to the very end, and twisted it around, and the feeling of *that*, as well as the feeling of having him lick my clitoris, was just about as much as I could bear. I had a climax, not a tremendously big one, but enough to make me shake. Phil held me very close, keeping his finger up my bottom the whole time, which kept giving me little aftershudders. Then he helped me off the car and we went into the house and straight up to the bedroom, and he made love to me, very slowly, because he knew that I had already been satisfied once.''

Just because there was a short interval of time in between the love play and the intercourse itself, that doesn't mean that what Phil and Susan did in the garage wasn't part of that eventual act of intercourse. The interval between love play and penetration can be even longer, provided the long-term intention is to carry out a satisfying act of love and that the intervening period is seen as part of the process of sexual arousal. Refraining from sex can sometimes be as erotically stimulating as having it, as the following example from Rickie, a 29-year-old cocktail hostess from San Francisco, more than vividly shows:

"Vinnie and I were flying back to San Francisco from seeing my mother in Van Nuys. Vinnie's my boyfriend, and my manager kind of. We were sitting at the back of the plane; it was dark because most people were sleeping. We had a whole row of seats to ourselves, and so I put up the armrests and rested my head on Vinnie's lap. He bent forward and kissed me and started stroking my arm. Then he started stroking my breast through my dress. I didn't mind. In fact, it was real relaxing, and my nipple stiffened up. So did Vinnie's penis; I could feel it against the back of my head. I turned my head around, and reached up, and tugged open his zipper, and reached my hand inside.

"His penis was real hard and hot, and it had that beautiful musky smell to it, you know when you open up a man's pants? Anyway I worked it out, right out of his zipper, and started to kiss it. I licked it all the way up and down, and put the tip of my tongue right into the hole at the end of his penis, and I could taste that first slippery sort of juice. That turned me on, so I opened my lips right up and took the whole of his penis into my mouth, and very gradually moved my head up and down, up and down, only using my lips, and sometimes licking him very fast with my tongue. I didn't hurry. There wasn't any need to. We had all the time in the world. He reached down with his hand and lifted up my dress and slipped his hand into my panties, and wriggled his finger into my pussy while I was sucking him; but all the time I was concentrating on *him.* We were almost landing when I felt his finger pushing deep into my pussy, and I could sense how tense his muscles were. He sprayed come all over my face, it was beautiful, and I took hold of his penis and used it to rub all that beautiful stuff all over my cheeks and my lips and my neck. It dried real quick, but I didn't wash it off.

"We sat in the back of the cab all the way from San Francisco Airport, all the way to Mill Valley, where we used to live, and all the time I could feel that tight sensation on my skin, and when I licked my lips I could taste come. It must have taken us maybe an hour to get home, maybe a little bit longer, but as soon as we got into the door we practically ran straight through into the bedroom and stripped off all of our clothes and we fucked. I promise you we fucked. It was delightful. All that pent-up feeling sitting in that cab came bursting out, and it was great."

When it comes to intercourse itself, your energy should be concentrated *internally* as much as externally, since the stimulation that you are seeking to experience is emotional as well as physical. Therefore, comfort is important, especially when you are high on the plateau phase of stimulation and approaching your orgasm.

In *How to Drive Your Man Wild in Bed*, I listed four different practical and comfortable intercourse positions, which are really all you need to know for years of completely fulfilling sex. These were simply man on top, you underneath; you on top, man underneath; side by side, man behind you; and one of the best of all intercourse positions, you on your back, man on his side beside you. Those four simple positions cover a multitude of incredible pleasures.

During the past decade, however, I have been asked by several women for a few variations of the basic theme. And now that women are generally so much fitter and more supple, there are some real possibilities for adapting the basic positions into several rather more adventurous ones. One of the best of these is an extension of the ordinary man-on-top– you- underneath missionary position. All you have to do as you lie on your back is raise your legs as high as you can until they are actually over your partner's shoulders. Then reach down with each hand and grasp the backs of your partner's thighs so that you are drawing him even deeper into you. This position restricts your movements. You are, after all, bent double, with your bottom in the air. But it increases the exposure of your vulva to your partner's thrustings, and he is able to push much more deeply into you with every stroke.

Then there are several standing-up positions, which can be exciting for a short while, especially if you are making love in the great outdoors or snatching a "quickie" in an elevator. The most practical is the one in which your partner lifts you up so that you are sitting in his lap, with his penis inside you, and your legs wrapped around behind his back. You should be resting most of your weight on the upper part of his thighs. If your balance and rhythm are mutual, you should be able to stay like that for quite a long time without tiring him.

An interesting position that requires reasonable fitness on your part is one in which your man sits on the bed, his legs apart, supporting himself with his arms. You then spread your legs and lower yourself onto his erect penis, with each of your legs over his thighs. You lean back on your hands in the same way that he is leaning back, and use the strength in your hands and your feet to lift yourself up and down on him. You can alter this position into a more intimate embrace simply by wrapping your legs around his waist and leaning forward to cuddle him. If he then leans forward too, he can put his hands underneath your bottom and lift you up and down on his penis.

The reason why I am generally not in favor of athletic or complicated positions is because they tend to turn sex into an Olympic performance, which it's not. They also increase the feeling that each act of love ought to be tremendously skilled and wonderfully successful. Anyone who has lived through a long-term sexual relationship knows that nobody is good in bed all the time. All kinds of unrelated problems can affect your sexual competence, from fatigue to illness to alcohol to stress. As long as you can talk freely to each other about your fears, your feelings, and your difficulties, then any anxieties or disappointments can be allayed right from the very moment they begin to develop.

If your man loses his erection right in the middle of making love to you and if he is unable to get it back again no matter how you administer to his penis with mouth or hands, then treat the problem lightly. If you begin to suggest that you turn him off, or give him the impression that there is something wrong with him, he will grow increasingly anxious about it, and the likelihood that he will fail to achieve an erection next time you make love will be that much higher.

Human beings are sexually very sensitive. So much of the sexual process depends on self-esteem and confidence and on the feeling that your partner shares your arousal and shares your pleasure. But both of you should understand that if one or the other of you doesn't happen to feel like making love one night, or if for some reason the mood is wrong, or the place is wrong, and intercourse isn't the grand combination of *Gone with the Wind* and *Chariots of Fire* that you expected it to be, then it isn't a personal insult or anything that could be considered a failure. It doesn't always work out, whatever you read in books or see in the movies. But if you can learn to enjoy the disappointments as well as the successes, then your long-term relationship will be deep, rewarding, and will eventually bring you the greatest erotic satisfactions of your life.

This is why I believe in treating lovemaking not just as series of isolated acts, but as a continuous, ongoing process. Sexual communication involves the daily expression to your man of your continuing desire to make love to him, even at times when actual intercourse is out of the question; even at times when neither of you actually feels like intercourse. If you can manage to communicate this feeling by your actions, your words, your kisses, and your affection, you will gradually build up a foundation of sexual security in your man's mind that when the time comes will enable him to make love to you strongly, confidently, and arousingly. He, of course, should be doing the same for you. There is no greater sexual stimulus than knowing that your partner is as aroused as you are.

In her self-help book *Having It All*, Helen Gurley Brown grades sexual experiences from the ecstatic to the mundane (albeit not too seriously), but in my opinion the less you see your sex life as a competition and the more you see it as a rounded, continuing experience, the more overall pleasure you are likely to derive from it.

We have talked about having sex in unexpected places, which can often give you a far higher erotic charge than usual. Sometimes suggest to your man that you follow the advice of that country and western song and lay the blanket on the ground and celebrate your mutual affection on it. Sex on the beach or in a forest, in a sauna or in a private swimming pool, add variety and fun to your long-term relationship, and above all they make your acts of love memorable.

Making sexual advances to your man at unusual times also adds a considerable frisson to your sex life. First thing in the morning, when he is still asleep, start kissing him and manipulating his penis. Tease him into waking up and making love to you then and there, even before he has opened his eyes. Be ready to make love as soon as he comes home from work; or allow yourself a little extra time next time you're getting dressed to go to dinner or the theater, and insist on making love to him just before you go.

Marjorie, 29, did: "My hair was beautifully curled, I had my makeup all done, my eyelashes on, and I looked fabulous. John was in the dressing room doing up his necktie. He hadn't yet zipped up his pants. So I came up behind him, and slipped down my robe, so I was naked except for my bra, and I reached inside his pants and took out his cock, and started to rub it until it was stiff. John said, 'Come on, Marjorie, we don't have time for that,' but I said, 'You don't think that I'm going to go out this evening and talk to all those other men without being able to think to myself that they don't know what *I* know, and that is that my cunt is full up with my husband's sperm?' Well, the idea of that really turned him on; and we lay down on the bedspread, and kissed each other, and got ourselves very superheated, and then we made love. And John was so affectionate to me that evening. I guess I'd given him reassurance, you know, as well as loving. For him, knowing that his sperm was inside me, that was a kind of secret ownership, this lady is mine.''

Jane, 31, annoyed and excited her husband in equal amounts by masturbating him while he was eating his breakfast, until he was so aroused that he had to put down his toast soldiers and make love to her on the dining room rug. He missed his commuter train that morning but agreed on the whole that the experience was worth it. Jane said, "I try very hard never to get into a rut with our sex life. Any time it seems as if it's getting stale, I try to do something surprising. Ben responds amazingly. In fact, if there's any competition in our marriage, it's about who can turn on the other one the most.''

Many women fail to realize that there is a great deal you can do *after* intercourse to enhance the experience and to demonstrate just how arousing you found it. In a way, it's like laying the foundations for the next act of love, showing that soon you will want more of the same, or better.

Remember that directly or intensely massaging your man's penis after sex can be irritating or even mildly painful, and that generally he will be sensitive (as you will be, too) to caresses that during buildup to intercourse were highly stimulating. All the same, you can very gently and systematically kiss him all over, all over his face, his neck, his shoulders, his chest, his stomach. When you reach his softened penis, carefully take hold of his testes and slip his penis into your mouth, licking the end of it around and around with the tip of your tongue. If his penis starts to stiffen, lick it a little more and then leave it, kissing his thighs and his hips but keeping your hands on his testes, manipulating them with extreme care. Then lie with your head on his hip, your mouth next to his penis, kissing it gently and occasionally sucking it, and pressing it up against your lips with the palm of your hand.

Remember that even when he is fully erect again, he will still be more sensitive than the first time you made love, so resist the temptation to start beating away at his penis with your hand as if you were pumping up a car tire. Now, still kissing and caressing his penis, turn yourself around so that you are on top of him, with your vulva directly over his face. Allow him to kiss and lick at your vagina and anus, but lift your hips away from him if his oral caresses become too persistent or too irritating. To my mind, it is *after* sex that the celebrated "69" position comes into its own; it is usually unsatisfactory when both partners are in a high state of sexual excitement because it allows neither of them to concentrate completely on achieving their own climax. After intercourse, however, when your mood is more relaxed, it is a very pleasant and gradually arousing experience, and it can often lead to a second act of intercourse within a very short space of time—shorter than usual.

You may not want to go as far as oral intercourse after having just made love. You may be too tired; you may already be deeply satisfied. But all the same, resist the temptation simply to kiss your man on the nose, roll over, and start snoring. Cuddle up close to his back, and unwind him by kissing him and tracing fingernail patterns lightly on his muscles. Occasionally, let your hands stray around to those sensitive areas around the backs of his thighs and his buttocks. Lightly cup his testes. Get to know his penis in repose as well as in a state of excitement. Above all, show that the descent from the summit, in its own gentle way, can be rewarding as the climb up there.

Another interesting after-sex technique is to sit on top of your lover and carefully guide his soft penis into your vagina. You will often find that he manages half an erection, and that will be sufficient for you gently to rise up and down on him and give him gentle, liquid stimulation with your very fluid insides. It is important to remember to control yourself: to restrain any urge to start jumping up and down on him violently. After-sex sex should be carried out with the greatest of gentleness and care, and should be seen as a "thank-you" rather than a "please." It is always much more than possible that a second or third act of intercourse will follow, but try not to regard that as the purpose or the ultimate goal of after-sex sex. Try to regard it instead as a quiet sharing of the satisfaction that you have enjoyed together. If you do happen to make love for a second or third time—well, count that as a bonus.

While we're on the subject of sexual intercourse, I should talk about anal intercourse, a variation that is becoming more and more popular among couples who are married or who are living together long-term and who are seeking not only different excitements but ways of continuing their sexual intimacies throughout the month.

In *How to Drive Your Man Wild in Bed*, I stressed that anal intercourse, provided it is sensibly carried out, is not dirty and not risky. Fecal matter does not enter the lower part of your bowel until you are actually ready to go to the john, as you can test for yourself when you are having a shower or a bath by soaping your middle finger and inserting it carefully into your anus, as far as it will go.

Anal intercouse can bring you great erotic rewards, since your rectum is rich with nerve endings that stimulate your entire genital area, and it should be almost as easy for you to reach a climax when your man makes love to you from the rear as it is when he makes love to you vaginally.

Too often, anal intercourse is painful or off putting because you are not adequately prepared for it. It is not a sexual variation that is advisable to try on the spur of the moment, although it tends to happen that way, when a couple have a little too much to drink or when they may be feeling sexually tense during the woman's period.

First, discover what you can do with your anus by privately spending some time touching it, probing it, and getting to be as familiar with it as any other part of your body. You will need a tube of some lubricant. Take a shower, paying particular attention to washing your vulva and your anus. Then towel yourself off, sprinkle yourself with powder, and find some comfortable place, like a bed or an armchair or a sofa, where you can hold a mirror in front of your open legs and see your anus clearly. Squeeze a liberal amount of jelly onto your finger, and massage it around your anus, gradually working the tip of your finger inside, as far as it will go. Then try inserting another finger and stretching your anus slightly.

There is a famous scene in the sex classic *L'Histoire d'O* in which the heroine is subjected to having hard rubber dildos pushed into her anus and chained into place, regularly having them removed to have progressively larger dildos inserted. You don't have to do anything as extreme as that, but as you grow more comfortable and more confident about inserting your fingers into your botton, try a small vibrator (they are usually marketed under the name of "Lady Fingers") or, if you are unable to find one or shy about buying one, try any similar object, such as a peeled zucchini, or a carrot, or a bottle with a suitable neck, provided it has no sharp edges on the cap. Just take the simple but important precaution of *never* inserting anything into your anus that may be gripped and broken off by your strong sphincter muscles. Apart from being dangerous, it can be extremely embarrassing to have to explain to the paramedics how you happened to fall over in the bathroom and accidentally sit on a bar of soap or whatever you have lost inside your rectum.

As you grow more and more relaxed, you will find that the best object for inserting into your anus is an ordinary vibrator, perhaps with a penis-shaped latex sleeve tugged over it. You should be able to push this right up inside your bottom (keeping a firm hold of the end of it), and the pleasures of letting it vibrate in your rectum are quite considerable. You might find that you like to insert a thrumming vibrator into your anus while you are actually making love to your husband or lover. Maybe he would like one in *his* too: The sensations he will feel will be just as delightful as yours. But the important point is not to be embarrassed about using your bottom as erotically as you use your vagina. Your anus can become a second sexual home for your lover's penis; and once you have become relaxed and adept in anal intercourse, you will find that your sex life can take on a whole new dimension.

Using a vibrator will gradually accustom your muscles to the sensation of having a large object pushed up inside your anus, and you will also be able to practice the technique of pushing and opening your anal muscles as your lover's penis approaches, rather than shrinking and tightening them, which will be your natural reaction.

There are some *don'ts* about anal intercourse. Don't persevere if your muscles really don't feel in the mood and his attempts to penetrate your anus cause you pain. That happens sometimes for no particular reason, and all you have to do is wait until the next time. *Don't* allow him to penetrate your anus and then immediately penetrate your vagina without washing himself thoroughly first. The chances are you will suffer an irritating vaginal infection as a consequence. *Don't* ever insert anything sharp, such as a pointed hairbrush handle or the long top of a nail varnish bottle, into your anus. The lining of the rectum is extremely elastic, but if it is punctured the results can be extremely serious.

Some women find that they can use their anuses as freely as their vaginas once they are capable of relaxing and enjoying the intense and unusual sensations that anal penetration can provide. Here's Sandy, 29, from Minneapolis: "When I was single, I always used to push something into my bottom to turn me on when I was masturbating. Usually, it was my thumb, but occasionally I used a pencil flashlight, and sometimes I would switch it on. It's incredible. I used to open my vagina with my fingers in front of the mirror, and I could see the glow of this flashlight shining red through the skin that seperates my vagina and my bottom. I did it for a boyfriend once, and he really freaked. He thought it was the sexiest thing that he'd ever seen in his life.

"When I met Jay, and started living with him, I used to continue to push my fingers up my bottom when we were making love, because that way I could always guarantee a climax. In the end, Jay began to realize that I liked having my bottom stimulated (which most women do, if only they would admit it), and we started having anal intercourse as well as vaginal intercourse. He could push his penis right up to the hilt into my asshole, and he always used to climax up inside me, so that in the morning the semen would come sliding out of my bottom. Sometimes I used to tell him to push his whole hand up into my vagina, and grasp his own penis through the skin between my vagina and my bottom, and masturbate himself using my skin like a glove. That used to excite me so much that I would scream out loud, but the sensation was so intense that I didn't encourage him to do it very often. I would have to be drunk or very frustrated to do anything that wild. But all I can say is that women shouldn't be shy about letting their lovers have sex with them that way. Men shouldn't be shy, either. I love to push my fingers up my boyfriend's ass when he's making love to me. He says it gives him a feeling like having his balls squeezed from the inside. He loves me, anyhow. He says I'm the most exciting thing that ever happened to him. And that can't be bad.''

During the numerous interviews I undertook for the preparation of this book, I even found a woman who regularly used to penetrate her husband anally while wearing a strap-on dildo. While this reversal of sexual roles may seem shocking to some people, both of them found balance and comfort in it, a sharing of sexual aggression. "It was marvelous, the first time I did it," she said. "I found I could push and push into him, and arouse him, just as if I were a man. Not that I felt like a man. I just shared some of the sexual power that I think a man feels when he makes love to a woman. And I think my husband shared some of the sexual submissiveness that a woman feels, the feeling of being penetrated and controlled, which is arousing in itself. He could lie there and allow himself to *be fucked,* if you'll excuse my language; and men can't usually experience that. It opened his eyes, you know. I'm sure it did. It certainly made him a gentler lover. More positive, but gentler."

If you have reservations about anal intercourse, don't keep them to yourself, discuss them with your lover. To begin with, it is an act that has to be undertaken with a high degree of mutual consent and a great deal of lubricant. But, eventually, if your early experiences of it are pleasant, you will find that it will become a natural and exciting part of your sexual repertoire.

The best positions for anal intercourse, especially for beginners, are (1) side by side, in the "spoons" position, with the man behind you. You can then ease your bottom back onto his penis and control the rate of penetration yourself; (2) doggie fashion, with you crouching on all fours on the bed, and your lover crouching over you; and (3) lady superior, with you on top of him while he lies on his back on the bed. You squat over him, guiding his erection into your anus with your own hand and then gradually sit down, allowing your own weight to drive his penis up into your anus.

Above all, it is your *attitude* to anal intercourse that will help you to enjoy it the most. Think of it calmly, in the same way as vaginal intercourse. If you feel a pang of muscular pain, don't overreact; that will only make it even more painful. Simply take a deep breath, relax, and allow the man you love to penetrate you where only the man you love is allowed to go.

Now that we have looked at intercourse, both straightforward and not so straightforward, we are ready to plunge into those variations that can really drive your man wild.

Let me say just one thing before we begin the next stage of this advanced primer into sexual excitement: Some of the sexual variations you will read about here will shock you and even repel you, even though they are fairly widely practiced. But always remember that the choice of what you do sexually is up to you. You can draw the line wherever you wish. You should never allow your partner to impose his sexual will on you, and he should never expect you to submit to practices that you find upsetting or frightening. You are an independent woman, and you have the right to make love in any way that comforts and excites and satisfies you, but you have no obligation to bend to the tastes of your sexual partner if they really offend you.

Also remember this, though: You and your man can enjoy many of the sexual practices that I am about to describe either by simply fantasizing about them or by trying a milder version of them. You can practice bondage, for instance, simply by tying your arms and ankles with scarves in a way in which they can easily be released. You will remember Louise, who fantasized about being chained up simply by gripping hold of the head of her bed. You may personally be aroused by allowing yourself to be totally at the mercy of your partner, in which case, please enjoy yourself to the utmost. But always make sure that you can trust that partner almost as much as you can trust yourself. Sexual variations should always be a mutual exploration of the remarkable sensations that the mind and the body are capable of experiencing. No sexual relationship can ever be pleasurable or successful on a long-term basis if it is being conducted solely to satisfy the sexual predilections of one partner alone.

With that in mind, let us now explore some of the wilder avenues of sexual stimulation.

11

Toys and Other Joys

Ten years ago, there were very few sexual aids on the market, apart from a small range of vibrators, a variety of fancy condoms, and some penis attachments that looked like dollhouse bathmats and were called "clitoral ticklers."

These days, anyone eager for varied stimulation can choose from hundreds of different products, plastic or leather, motorized or hand cranked, as well as all sorts of extraordinary items of erotic clothing. To be quite honest, very few of these products are worth the money you will be expected to pay for them. But now and again it doesn't do you any harm to experiment with one or two erotic novelties, and I certainly wouldn't want to dissuade you from trying anything that tickles your fancy (or your clitoris).

To begin with, let's take a look at vibrators, which for a woman are the most useful of all sexual artifacts. A typical advertisement for a vibrator announces, "A viciously effective stimulator (available in black or white) as favored by the ladies of the Brazilian aristocracy. Its unique snakelike action mercilessly activates the nerve endings of the vaginal orifice, nerves that are bypassed by the conventional vibrator which is active only at the tip. This unique action also stimulates the lubrication duct and women who thought they knew themselves well report a massive increase in fluid emission after just a few moments alone with the vibrating penis. It is contoured according to the penis of a donkey which has more pleasure-giving ridges and bumps than the human penis but it is sensibly proportioned at 7½ inches long." And, by golly, this amazing vibrator is on offer for only $7.

It's interesting to note that in the same magazine another vibrator was being advertised (allegedly by a different company) as having "a unique snakelike action" and being shaped "according to the penis of the Aztec warriors, who had more pleasure-giving bumps and ridges than Europeans—but is sensibly sized at 7½ inches." Obviously Aztec warriors were slightly more arousing than donkeys, because the price of the vibrator is $8.25.

Then there is the Pleasure Penis, which is not motorized but is simply a large latex dildo, often available with a squeeze bulb that you can fill with specially provided cream in order to simulate a male ejaculation. These products come with a variety of lubricants—Joy Jelly, Motion Lotion, or Oral Jelly, all of which are mildly flavored jellies for rubbing on your vagina during intercourse or oral sex. Personally, I prefer the flavor of vagina to the flavor of strawberry or mint, but in many cases the action of smoothing on the lubricant can be a stimulant in itself.

Other creams and sprays include Action Cream for women, which you are supposed to massage into the genital area before sex (that alone should turn you on). Then there is Special Cream for lubricating the vagina, Beauty Bust Cream for massaging into your breasts before sex, and even Orgasm

Cream, which you rub furiously into your clitoris and is supposed to help you reach a climax (and why not?).

Vibrators come in all shapes and sizes—not only Aztec or donkey style. There are Love Eggs, which are motorized egg-shaped vibrators from Sweden, based on the ancient Chinese *ben-wa.* You insert the entire egg into your vagina, lie back, and switch on the motor; the egg gently thrums you toward an orgasm. The *ben-wa,* incidentally, were weighted ivory balls joined together by a silken cord, which Chinese ladies inserted into their vaginas and then rocked backward and forward in order to enjoy the eccentric oscillating effect inside them. You can buy plastic *ben-wa* today, but I am told by a lady expert that they do not have quite the same effect as the hand-carved ivory variety.

There are anal poles—attachments that fit over the top of conventional vibrators. These can be simple pencillike rods of latex, or they can sport fringed tops like palm trees or stippled sides, depending upon how much stimulation you require. There is even a motorized anal finger, which you simply push up your anus while you are making love to your man, and allow to buzz while you work.

One Swedish manufacturer sells a very discreet "travel-kit" for women in a luxurious case, which includes a powerful seven-inch vibrator with a latex sleeve in the shape of a penis, a vibrating egg, and two different kinds of vaginal lubricants. Smaller vibrators are advertised as being of "pocketbook size." There is even a breast massager, a vibrating plastic cup into which you place your breast (nipple exposed) and that is guaranteed to keep your bust in "kissable condition." Price: $15.

For men, and particularly for men without women, there are several varieties of battery-operated vaginas "incorporating realistic moisture from spongy sleeve within." There are also numerous sex dolls, some of them (like Hot Cherry and Sexy Doreen) inflatable. Hot Cherry is "hot, ripe, and waiting just for you." She is a "beautiful, blue-eyed doll that can be yours to keep forever, with a fantastic 38–26–36 body and a perfectly formed vagina." Then there is the German Rubber Lady (De-Luxe) to whom "no illustration would do justice." She has a lifelike mouth, vagina, and anus. She has real hair, lips, fingernails, etc. Some disreputable shops are selling her for over $2,000, but you can buy her for $500.

The clitoral stimulators are still with us, although they have become more elaborate as time has gone by. These "ticklers" are soft latex rings that your man is supposed to put around the base of his penis and that feature a raised cock's comb of small latex bumps. These are intended to rub against your clitoris while you are making love and bring you to a quicker orgasm.

As we have seen from the earlier chapters on your sexual anatomy, your clitoris hides itself just before you reach a climax, and so this kind of artificial stimulation is not only unnecessary but can be irritating. Ticklers don't cost very much: only about $5. But you can have just as much pleasure without them and spend your $5 on something else.

Generally, it seems to me that sexual aids are overrated. Sometimes they add a little excitemnt to an evening's sex; but most of the time they turn out to be a disappointment. Unless they are very straightforward and practical, like the basic vibrator and its various attachments, they tend to be uncomfortable and even painful. I do, however, recommend the vibrator, particularly if you are keen to explore your own body and practice your sexual responses. Time and time again, women have told me that they find vibrators useful, discreet, satisfying, and helpful. Certainly they can help you explore yourself sexually, your feelings, and your responses, not to mention your nervous tolerances, in the absence of a man. Vibrators have no emotional hang ups and no egos, so you can use them whenever and wherever you want without recrimination.

Kathy is 28, married, and owns two vibrators, with the full knowledge and approval of her husband. "I don't use them very often; mostly when Lennie's away on business. But occasionally during the day I feel like sitting down on the couch, and reading one of those sexy romantic novels, and arousing myself. Then I use my vibrators. One of them is really big, ten inches long, with a rubber sleeve in the shape of a man's penis. The other is smaller, with bumps on the sides. I start off by switching the large vibrator on, and rubbing it slowly and gently against my clitoris, just to feel the buzz; then when I start to get aroused I slide it inside, and gradually work it up and down until it starts to push right against my womb.

"I don't always use both of them. It depends how I feel. But if I'm really worked up, I'll moisten my bottom with the lubricant from my vagina, and push the smaller vibrator into my anus. With the two of them buzzing inside me together, the sensation can sometimes be fantastic. I fantasize a lot when I'm doing it; I'll create fantasies; and quite often I'll use those fantasies again when I'm making love to Lennie. Lennie knows that I use the vibrators every now and then. Once or twice, I've used them on him. He doesn't object at all; in fact he thinks they're a part of our sex life. They don't talk back, after all; and I'm not about to marry one and run off and leave my family, so there isn't any need for Lennie to feel threatened."

Some feminists object to vibrators on the grounds

that they are an embodiment of the way in which men sexually dominate women: the almighty and dictatorial phallus. But the way I see it, they are nothing more than mechanical devices that help you explore the shape and the sensations of your vagina. When you are using a vibrator, you are in complete control of it, and it is your nerve endings that are important, not the shape of the device you are using to stimulate them. On the other side of the coin, I have never noticed even the most macho men complaining about artificial vaginas.

I also classify erotic underwear as sex toys. After all, they are the clothes you dress up in to play your erotic games. You have probably seen the kind of nylon frillies that are sold by Frederick's of Holly-wood and their many imitators—bras with holes for your nipples to protrude through, G-strings, wasp-waisted basques, garter belts, crotchless panties—there are dozens of underwear companies catering to what I call the French maid syndrome. There is no doubt that many men respond very favorably to seeing their wives or their lovers dressed up in sexy fragments of brightly colored see-through nylon.

If you are not particularly enthused by the French maid look and want to wear something that is more in keeping with being a modern and independent lady, there are all kinds of underwear that are equally sexy but much more practical and simple. Many clothing companies are now marketing feminine versions of male jockey shorts, with broad elasticated waistbands and in plain solid colors. On a woman, they can look extremely sexy. The G-string, which used to be worn only by strippers, is now a common part of almost every modern woman's wardrobe. A French underwear manufacturer to whom I spoke on Rodeo Drive in Los Angeles told me that backless panties now account for almost a third of his sales in Europe. He showed me an exquisite G-string made of almost transparent silk and decorated with pale shell-colored silk stitching. "If a woman wants to wear a pair of well-fitting slacks, she has no alternative," he said. "Besides, a woman looks beautiful in a small *cache sex* like this; the apex of femininity."

At the same highly exclusive store in which I met the French designer, one of the lady sales assistants told me that not only was underwear becoming sexier, sometimes it just wasn't there at all. She estimated that over a quarter of her lady customers, when they changed to try on dresses, were nude underneath their street clothes. Of course, it's rather more comfortable walking around Rodeo Drive on a spring morning dressed (or undressed) like that; walking along West Good Hope Road, Milwaukee, on a fall afternoon is something different. The lady assistant didn't think that her ladies went naked under their dresses for the particular purpose of pleasing men. She saw it instead as a newly relaxed attitude toward nudity and an assertion of their self-confident femininity.

Another aspect of modern womanhood she noticed was the almost wholesale removal of pubic hair. Obviously, she said, the fashion for high-sided Christie Brinkley style swimsuits had led to many women being obliged to shave off some or all of their pubic hair, and it seems to now be regarded as fashionable and clean and normal. The number of new depilatory products on the market specifically for the removal of genital hair seems to bear her observations out. Bikini Bare is selling well all over the country, even in places where it's too cold to wear a bikini.

Fiona, 23, a secretary from San Francisco, told me: "I first shaved off my pubic hair when I started wearing a bikini. I wasn't very hairy, it didn't show out of the sides of my swimsuit or anything like that, but I just preferred it. I started just by shaving the sides, but then I thought what's the difference and I shaved it all off. And I do it regularly now, without even thinking about it. My boyfriend adores it. He went wild when he first saw me shaved. We were going out to a party, and he went so stiff he couldn't get his jeans on. We had to make love just so that he could get dressed. He still loves it just as much. He says he loves the feel of it, and I get more oral sex these days than I can manage. He's always wanting to do down on me and suck me out. He loves to kiss my bare lips; and I have to admit that I like him doing it."

It appears to me that a taste for women with shaven vulvas is much more widespread among men than I previously would have imagined. In fact, the taste is strong enough to warrant an exceptionally high-selling sex magazine in Scandinavia that is devoted entirely to shaved models. Casual look-through magazines like *Playboy* or *Penthouse* show that even the girl next door types in which they specialize have been industrious supporters of Mr. Gillette. In a very informal survey, I asked sixty different men from all walks of life—from publishers to advertising agencies to accountants to garage attendants—what they would think if their wives or girlfriends shaved off their pubic hair. Some blushed, some laughed, some said positively not, but out of sixty men, over forty said they would like it very much. And that to me is quite a high percentage.

All I can say to you is this: Why not try it? If your lover doesn't like it all that much, you will find that your pubic hair very quickly grows back again. If it drives him as wild as my small informal survey seems to suggest it will, then it will certainly pay dividends in bed. You could even persuade him to shave off his, too, like the couple I met in Sweden who used to perform sex on stage at the celebrated Chat Noir club. "Inge and I both shaved ourselves very early on in our relationship. We wouldn't dream now of letting the hair grow back again. The sensation of closeness when you have intercourse is incomparable. When I think of all the people in the Western world who are making love through a tangle of hair, I feel almost sorry for them. They don't know what they're missing."

If you do consider shaving any or all of your pubic hair, do remember to take the basic precautions of using a clean razor with a new blade, and do use plenty of soap and water in order to avoid "nicking" the skin, which can give you cuts or irritating spots. Trim the hair down short with nail scissors first, then carefully shave it. Wash your vulva thoroughly afterward. When your hair starts to grow back, avoid the irritation of stubble by using a proprietary depilatory cream.

Beyond the usual run of sex toys and erotic clothing, there are strange and specialized garments and devices in rubber and leather. These are the manifestation of the moment when erotic games and erotic fantasies converge and become reality.

As you have seen, you can play out your sexual fantasies in many ways: in your head, as a game without props, as a fully fledged performance with chains to bind you and whips to keep you in order.

There is nothing wrong or perverted about using any kind of device in order to enhance your sexual arousal, no matter how startling it may sound. But in order to make your erotic experiences with rubber and leather both safe and happy, you should observe certain fundamental precautions and *never* attempt to bend or stretch them. This is simply a question of personal safety. The very last thing I am trying to do is turn you off, because you will frequently find that a little mild dabbling into the

world of rubber and restraint is highly exciting and
that it will turn your man on in ways that you didn't
imagine possible.

Exactly why some people are sexually excited by
rubber and leather and the idea of being tied up is
still impossible to say with any certainty. The
Dutch sex dominatrix Monique von Cleef once told
me that many of her clients were leading businessmen, even a police chief, who came to be tied up and
spanked and dressed in rubber masks simply to escape the heavy responsibility of their jobs and to as-
suage their guilt at always having to tell people
what to do. Monique may or may not be right, but
there is no question that some men do find bondage
and rubber very arousing and that your marriage or
long-term relationship could benefit from just a seasoning of it.

If you suspect that your husband or lover is more
than mildly interested in fetishistic clothing and
bondage, how can you broach the subject? Again,
the answer is careful communication. Tell him that
a friend of yours at work frequently gets tied up to
the bedposts by her husband and that she says she
loves it. Ask him if he would like to try it with you. If
there is no response whatsoever, let the matter
drop. He may either be reticent about showing any
enthusiasm, or he may simply not be interested. If
he is reticent, he may bring it up again later.

If he is interested, however, question him further.
Ask him if he thinks rubber is erotic. But say it
straightforwardly. Don't wrinkle up your nose and
say, ''I don't know what people see in rubber, do
you?'' Because if he *does* have a slight fetish for rubber or leather, that kind of preemptive disapproval
will put him off straight away; you may never find
out the truth and, still worse, you may never get the
sexual benefit of sharing his tastes with him.

Some of the sexual garments you can buy for enjoying yourself in rubber and leather are *extremely* extreme, and you would have to be a fully fledged fetishist to enjoy them. But many of them can be used by quite normal, balanced, well-adjusted couples who are looking for nothing else but a few evenings of unusual fun.

A Danish company produces an entire sexual range in latex, including dozens of different pairs of latex briefs with hard rubber dildos inside them, both for men and women, both vaginal and anal. They have latex bras with holes for your nipples, latex Bermuda shorts with open crotches, latex whips (with phallic handles) for the sauna, latex aprons, special latex masks with protruding rubber tongues for cunnilingus, and latex masks with inflatable rubber penises inside that can be blown up completely to gag the wearer.

It is when we start straying into the area of gagging and restraint that the strict rules about bondage and fetishism start to apply. Absolute rule number one, before any other rule, is that you should never attempt any kind of bondage or unusual sexual activity with a man you don't know very well and can't trust implicitly. The sense of that rule is obvious. The second rule is that both partners should agree that if either one of them wants to stop the game or be released from his or her restraints or gags at any moment, no matter what the circumstances, they should be released immediately. Personally, I am very much against the use of gags or breathing restraints of any kind during sex (or at any other time), and I would advise you not to get involved in that particular scene. The point is that for many people, particularly men, restricting their breathing during masturbation or intercourse can actually intensify their climaxes, but the risks far outweigh the potential thrills. A young journalist I knew well died at the age of 17 because he suffocated himself with a rubber bathcap while masturbating; and the same thing happens to countless men and a lesser number of women every year.

The third rule is that you should never be tempted to leave either yourself or your partner alone in your house or apartment while in bondage. The amusing side of that situation is exemplified by the story of the Pan American hostess who left her boyfriend chained naked in their closet while she flew to Baltimore for the day, only to find that her plane was grounded by fog and that she would be unable to return to let him loose. Police eventually had to break into his apartment and release him, deeply red faced, of course.

The less amusing side of it is illustrated by the true story of the man who mailed his padlock key to himself, then bound himself up in the hallway of his apartment, locking himself with his padlock. The idea was that the postman would deliver his key the next day, he would release himself, and that would be that. But an unofficial postal strike delayed the return of the key for four days, and by the time it eventually arrived the man was almost dead from exposure and starvation. Sex—even fetishistic sex—is supposed to be fun; and that is why you should make a point of staying away from anybody who suggests you should do anything as *outré* as that. You should always be in control or, at the very least, in the control of somebody you can trust beyond any shadow of a doubt to take absolute care of you.

Leather garments tend to be more reminiscent of the Middle Ages. You can still buy a chastity belt, leather ankle shackles, or straps for buckling your wrists to your thighs or even to your ankles. I have seen full horse harnesses for women, complete with bits, advertised in a respectable publication, and chastity belts for men, too, with heavy womanproof locks on them. Of all the leather-bondage apparatuses I have seen, as most notable for women I would select a leg spreader, which is a long steel bar that is strapped to each ankle, preventing you from closing your legs. For men I would choose an extraordinary device called the Five Gates of Hell, which is a series of tight leather straps that buckle around the shaft of his penis. The topmost strap has a chain attached to it, which in turn is connected to a strap around his neck, so that his penis is permanently forced to rear up.

By far the most extraordinary sexual device I have ever seen is a kind of face mask/hookah. I didn't understand what it was at first, but it was later explained to me that it was a device for obliging a man to take every breath bubbled through his mistress's urine. I have to admit that with all my experience of erotic peculiarities, I did consider this device beyond the limit. But—there you are—we all have different limits; and provided you feel secure and happy and comfortable when you are making love to your man, there should be no limit at all to what you feel you can do with him. It is up to you to decide—not me, not society, not the opinions of your friends. Explore your sexual relationship with him just as far as you want to go, because then you will continually please and amuse him.

While we're on the subject of wet sex or golden showers, which are terms for the use of urine in sexual games, we might as well make a few points about it. For many woman, orgasm is quite frequently accompanied by the involuntary passing of a small amount of urine. If that happens to you, you should never be ashamed of it or worried about it. Instead, make it part of your sexual activities. Keep a towel underneath you to protect the bed or couch, but use that small squirt of urine as a manifest expression of your sexual joy. Massage your man's penis with it as part of your after-sex pleasuring; you can always wash your hands afterward.

Linda Lovelace once described the wet-sex games she played, which are typical of the urinary splashings in which many thousands of American couples occasionally indulge themselves. But when Linda wrote about them ten years ago they were still considered taboo.

"You might try this next time you're feeling adventuresome," she said. "That's peeing inside a woman's pussy. There can sometimes be a problem keeping a hard-on while peeing, but it's been done to me many times. In the morning is a good time for this, when the man wakes up with what is referred to as a piss hard-on. The cleanest way to do it is for the woman to sit on the toilet with her pussy lips parted wide. He kneels between her legs, puts it in, and lets it flow. The sensation is terrific for the woman—this I know. The stream of hot pee feels great as it washes your insides, and there's something kind of pleasant about the sound of it dripping out of you. Men like it too."

And here is an excerpt from a letter I received from Mandy, who lives in Peoria, Illinois. Mandy is 26 and a dance instructor. "My boyfriend Hal and I took a shower together recently, and while we were kissing and cuddling and letting the water gush all over us, Hal said that he had to step out and take a pee. I told him not to bother, he could do it in the shower, we could soon wash ourselves clean. So I held his cock, and he just peed, straight upwards, a hot bubbling stream of it, and I found that it excited me. I directed it over my stomach, and over my breasts, and then between my legs. We were both of us so excited that we did it again next time we were in the shower, and this time I knelt down and let him pee all over my face and hair, so that I was soaked in it; and I was so aroused that I started to pee, too.

"After that, we did it maybe two or three times a week, almost every time that we bathed together, and I just loved rubbing his urine all over my body, and last week I opened my mouth and let him pee straight into my mouth, although I didn't swallow any, I simply took a mouthful and spurted it out again. Straight afterwards Hal got down and closed his mouth over my cunt and I peed straight down his throat, and he said that he adored it."

Mandy was worried whether her water sports with Hal might be unhygienic and also lead to regular fetishistic behavior. The answer to both questions is basically no. Most couples who discover thrills of wet sex usually find that it is a passing fad and that it quickly loses its initial erotic "naughtiness." A great deal of the stimulation it provides is childish, in the sense that a private act that they have associated since early childhood with being "dirty" and "wrong" is now permissible, and not only permissible but pleasurable.

As far as the question of hygiene is concerned, the shower is obviously an ideal place to play wet sex games, since you can wash directly afterward; but urine is sterile as it emerges from the urethra, and so there is no risk of poisoning. I would, however, recommend that you don't actually drink it, at least not in large quantities. If you decide like Mandy that your man can give you a high-pressure hosing, then take a quick wash and gargle with mouthwash soon afterward.

Brian and Fay, a young couple from New York, went through two or three months of wet sex during the summer of 1982. They would often go out into the woods upstate simply to pee and make love in the great outdoors. "I used to love to pee standing up, naked except for my panties," said Fay. "I would pee right through my panties, and Brian would hold his hand between my legs and enjoy every last burst of it.''

Wet sex is certainly less arduous or risky than spanking, which is another very powerful male sexual predilection. There *are* women who get aroused when their bottoms are spanked, but not nearly as many as those men who get turned on by the sight of a flaming crimson pair of buttocks would like to believe. If your husband or lover likes to inflict pain in any way and you dislike the idea of being paddled or whipped, then obviously you have a divergence of sexual interests that is going to be extremely difficult for you to overcome. This is because there is one area in which women have won equal rights over the past ten years—even superior rights—and this unquestionably is the area of sexual relationships. No man has any right or justification to make you do anything sexual against your will; not kissing, not petting, not intercourse, not bondage, not whipping, not anything. Your own body is your own, even if you have been living with your man for forty years, and you are entitled to protect your sexual integrity against any kind of physical or emotional browbeating.

I have discussed the sex toys and games in this chapter with one thing in mind: that you will be able better to understand the variety or urges and inclinations that men can have, even men who in every other way appear to you to be very conventional and respectable. Men are far more *visual* in their sexual responses and far more *mechanical*, too. They are far less emotionally inhibited by the idea of tying somebody up or wearing some highly sexual item of clothing. Almost all pornography is bought by men, which (since pornography is equally available to women) shows how different their sexual responses generally are.

You can, however, use you man's maleness to your own advantage. For instance, if he evinces an interest in spanking or slightly sadistic behavior, you can suggest that he buy himself a sado-masochistic (s/m) video, which you can run through together while he makes love to you in a more conventional way. By doing this, you will show that you understand his tastes and that you are prepared to accept them and even help him to fulfill them, but that you do not personally want to be spanked or whipped or otherwise punished, not in the name of sexual satisfaction.

Most sex stores carry a line of s/m videos or will be able to tell you where they can be acquired. A fairly typical example is this: "This film is about five young people, three girls and two men, having one thing in common. They can only get orgasm and ejaculation by sexual violence and rape. One of the girls can only get her orgasm when being tied up and then whipped, the other wants to be hung up somehow, and thereafter to be screwed violently, while the third one claims to be in contact with leather and to have rings in both her nipples and her cunt lips."

The brochure came from Germany, and the title of the film is "Bizarre Life."

Most sexual predilections are catered to by pornographic magazines and videos. One of my standard words of advice to women who are concerned that their husbands or lovers have slightly unusual sexual tastes that they themselves do not feel they can adequately satisfy is to encourage their men to buy whatever pornography they want, and to read it or watch it together, while making love in a way that is more acceptable to them than what is happening on the screen. The results of this advice appear so far to have worked exceedingly well.

One lady teacher from Chicago told me with relief

that her husband seemed to be more than satisfied with watching videos like "Leather-Bound Slave-girl" while making love to her and that he no longer dropped hints about tying her up. The point about pornography is that it need not be feared: It amounts to nothing more than extreme fantasies depicted by models in photographs or on film, and it is a defuser of sexual tensions, rather than a stimulant. All you have to worry about with sex is the fear of sex itself, and if you can show your husband or lover that you understand his particular tastes, that you understand that they are nothing more than erotic fantasies, and that you are prepared to enjoy them with him on paper and on film, then you will discover that entire areas pf sexual anxiety are suddenly calm and safe and manageable.

"I found a whole collection of sex magazines in my husband's desk, all full of people doing everything imaginable. My first reaction was to feel upset, even jealous, and betrayed. But then I thought to myself: These are only magazines. They must turn him on, or he wouldn't have bought them. But they're no threat to me. They're only pictures. Probably the only reason he hasn't shown them to me is because he's embarrassed. So what I did was go out and buy him a sexy magazine myself, and give it to him, and that night we read it in bed together, and the result was that we made love beautifully. He was so relaxed, it was almost as if some weight had been taken off his mind, and he was much more enthusiastic and exciting in bed than he normally is. I think that any wife who feels jealous or upset about her husband looking at pornography is just as silly as a mother who finds a copy of *Playboy* under her teenage son's pillow and gets upset about that. Men look at sex differently, that's all; and I think that any woman who can understand that can have the happiest sex life imaginable, don't you?"

That was Kate, 31, a sensible and well-educated housewife and a one-time teacher from Indianapolis. Kate understood that pornography rarely amounts to more than a vicarious thrill and that it improves long-term relationships far more often than it undermines them. A man who reads pornography, no matter how extreme it might appear, is no more likely to go out and commit the acts depicted on the pages of his magazines than a crime novel enthusiast is likely to go out and murder somebody.

There is, of course, another problem to think about. Does pornography insult and degrade the female sex? If you look through pornography with your husband and lover, are you aiding and abetting the male exploitation of female sexuality? As one feminist said to me, "I would no more allow my daughter to look at pornography with her lover than I would allow her to go out on the streets with him and push drugs. Unlike drugs, pornography isn't criminal, but something doesn't have to be criminal to be dangerous."

This lady felt the same way about sex aids, vibrators, love eggs, and "anything and everything that dehumanizes the female body."

I don't personally agree that pornography degrades either those who appear in it or those who read it or view it. Much of it is sleazy and unattractive, but there are sleazy and unattractive things in every area of human life. There are sleazy and unattractive restaurants, but their existence is no excuse for closing down all restaurants. Pornography to me is just one aspect of the wide and varied world of human sexuality, which can be tender and beautiful, vicious and crude, creative and dirty all at the same time.

I have worked in Scandinavia with porno models and found most of them to be humorous, well-balanced, and happy, with an extremely realistic and constructive view about sex. "If what I am doing makes men and women feel less self-conscious about sex; if it arouses them; then I think I must be doing some good," said Birgitta, 21. Did she feel degraded by appearing in films and magazines with her legs wide open, displaying her vagina? "Why should I feel degraded? The first time I opened up a magazine and saw myself with my pussy showing, I was very satisfied. The only person who was upset was my father. I am a pretty girl, I know that I am pretty, and what is the harm in displaying what is most beautiful about the female body." But what about pictures of intercourse and pictures in which she has objects thrust inside of her? "It makes no difference. Sexual excitement— what do you call it?—*uplifts* people. Makes them feel happy. You can give no greater gift to yourself or to other people than happiness."

In sum, you should take the trouble to find out if there are any particular sexual quirks that excite the man in your life and then see how far you can happily go to satisfy and fulfill them. You may want to try sex toys; you may want to try sexy videos; you may want to dress up as a nurse in a rubber apron. In the commercial world of sex toys and sexual clothing, there is something for everyone, with a price list to match.

The key is, to drive your man wild or wilder in bed, try anything once. You may discover that something that once repelled you is a great deal more exciting and attractive than you thought and you can open up a whole new dimension of erotic excitement for both of you.

Georgina, 22, could never understand the appeal of rubber. "I thought it was just one of those kinky things that people liked. It didn't do anything for me at all." But then her live-in boyfriend bought her a pair of latex briefs, and she began to understand what it was about rubber that turns some people on. "I'd never be a rubber freak, or anything like that. But it's very clinging and very silky and it has an extraordinary kind of an aroma to it. It's extremely hard to describe what it does. It's like a second skin."

Georgina bought one or two more garments, a latex bra and a pair of dance pants with a penis insertion, and that was all she felt she wanted. "I don't wear them very often, but sometimes I feel like it. I mean, people indulge themselves in every other possible way, why shouldn't they indulge themselves when it comes to sex? Sex doesn't even make you fat."

12

How to Give Him the Affair He's Always Wanted

He's caught your eye across that crowded room—
you've gone across to him and used your coming on
strong technique in order to charm and disarm him.
He invites you to come and have dinner with him at
a table for two with candles and moonlight and
Gypsy violinists—or maybe a pot roast at his mother's, with *Taxi* on the television—but you know you
like him, you know you want to see more of him,
you suspect very much that you want to go to bed
with him. What should you do?

It's all very well being a strong, independent,
feminist-type career lady, but how does that affect
your standing with the man of your erotic dreams?
Just because you can now assert yourself at work,
does that mean that you can assert yourself equally
in your personal relationships? If you suggest going
to bed together, is he going to think that you're
pushy? Or a pushover? Will he respect you? How
will it affect your relationship if you start calling the
shots from the very beginning? How can you be
feminine and independent and happy, too?

Although I have advocated coming on strong as a
successful technique for getting to know and in-

trigue those men who attract you strongly across those crowded rooms, it is worth remembering that assertiveness does not always equal strength. In sexual affairs, too, assertiveness can be a real turn off, particularly if the man of your choice is looking forward to conquering you and carrying you off to his castle. There are times when a little shyness and innocence and helplessness work wonders, as long as you privately make sure that you keep very secure control on everything that's happening.

Let's take the office affair, which for the career lady is the most frequent kind. You meet your new boss— you're attracted to him at once. He's very good-looking, with brown hair, melting eyes, and is also the owner of one of the most arousing asses you've ever seen enclosed in a pair of Davide Cenci slacks.

Or, these days, it just as often happens that *you're* the boss and *he's* the secretary. In that event a whole different set of social and sexual rules apply. If you're the boss, you will, of course, have the advantage of a high degree of everyday influence over him. If he values his job, he's going to treat you extra nice. But the disadvantage is that having an affair with their lady bosses can tend to emasculate some men and consequently you could be robbed of the natural pleasures of having an affair with a man who behaves as assertively as a man should, both *in* bed and *out* of it. Is he going to tell you the truth about the way you look and the way you make love if he's anxious that you might summarily sack him in pique? Can you really enjoy a relationship in which you have the ultimate upper hand? Some ladies can; others find that they prefer the security of a man who is independent and can make his social and sexual judgments without fear of what they, the ladies, might think.

First, let's take the situation where *he's* the boss. From the very outset, you're going to have to accept that the minute you start fooling around with him, your job is going to be at risk. If you prefer your job to the chance of a few months' pleasure, then have the self-discipline to hold off. Go seduce your local librarian instead. Office affairs hardly ever stay secret, and if your boss is married or has competitors for his job, then he's going to be under constant stress, not only from his family situation, not only from his upwardly mobile and competitive colleagues, but from *you*, too. Because no matter how good you think you are for him, no matter how much you see yourself as someone with whom he can retreat from the disagreeable realities of everyday life, he's going to regard you as one more pressure in a life that is already full of pressure. The time may come when that pressure gets too much for him to handle, and then he's going to have to make a choice, among you, his wife, his job. I've been down that road myself, and I know from firsthand experience what that pressure is like. It can damage a man's status at the office forever; it certainly affects the quality of his work.

Not that I'm trying to suggest that you *shouldn't* have an affair with your boss. Scores of boss–secretary relationships, even though they may have to be tested in the crucible of divorce and job loss, turn out to be happy and successful and very long-term relationships. I'm not a subscriber to the view that you should chicken out of life just because there might be problems ahead. The most exciting and rewarding relationships are always those that have been won against the odds.

Anyway, you've met your boss; you've been positive and up front with him; you've won his interest. Now what should you do? You should be efficient, of course, and not allow your feelings for him to affect your work. After all, you want to show him that you're capable and that he can rely on you. Don't overdo it, though. I know some secretaries who spend all their time making their bosses cups of coffee and running personal errands for them, and although every secretary's job involves a certain amount of that kind of gofering, you shouldn't allow yourself to be too much of a messenger girl. Show some independence, particularly in the way you run your own office and your own work and in the way you speak to him. Be critical of him now and again, like ribbing him for wearing that red tie with that blue shirt. If he's a bachelor, he'll begin to rely on your opinion, particularly when it comes to personal matters; if he's married, he'll begin to wonder why his wife let him leave the house looking like that. Study the job that he's doing; get to know what it's all about, and now and again ask him to explain some aspect of it to you. Sit close while he does so; don't be afraid to show him that you're physically interested.

You have shown him that you are capable, clever, and dependable. You have shown him that you have an independent head on your shoulders, so that in the event of a crisis between you, you will be able to fend for yourself and you won't be a burden on him. This, of course, is a feeling of security that comes express parceled from Fool's Paradise. If you *do* have a romance with him and he falls for you deeply enough to create any kind of marriage or career crisis, then the greatest burden on him is going to be his affection and loyalty for you, no matter how independent you are. But it will encourage him to start dating you, and that's all that we have to worry about for now.

Start involving him in your personal life by explaining some of your interests and problems to him. Ask his advice on private matters, like what should you say to a man friend of yours whose girlfriend is pregnant (never mind if you've really got a man friend whose girlfriend is pregnant). If he still hasn't asked you out for a drink or dinner, there's no harm in you asking him, even if he's married, to come to a small cocktail party at your apartment, maybe on his way home from work. You'd be surprised how many men in their early thirties, particularly those who have been married for a while, have forgotten that romantic feeling of dating and going to parties and simply being infatuated with a girl. They act mature, they act staid, they act responsible, but under that fudsy exterior beats the excited heart of a little boy.

Once you have dated your boss socially, you may find that things happen very rapidly indeed. Outside of the office, he will take a much more personal look at you. His eyes will refocus, and instead of Miss Doe, the smart and efficient secretary, he will suddenly see a pretty, independent young woman with a mind of her own; a woman with taste and style and looks. If he has invited you out to dinner, the chances are that he's going to expect to take you to bed at the end of the evening. If you've invited him to a party, the chances are that he's going to expect you to take him to bed at the end of the evening.

I know you're going to ignore this advice. You're not going to be thinking about this book as you stare into his melting brown eyes across that candlelit table, you mind giddy with too much Château Lafite Rothschild, his warm muscular hand resting on yours, the violinist playing "Roses in Your Teeth." You're going to say *yes* when it is very important for you at this point to say *no*. But even if you only say no on the first date, say no.

You don't have to give him an excuse. No woman is obliged to give any excuse to any man at any time to explain why she doesn't want to go to bed with him. But if you do feel compelled to say something, simply tell him that you need to think; or that you never make love on a first date; or that you're expecting a call from you cousin in New South Wales, Australia, and that you have to sit by the phone.

This is the time when you can act innocent and defenseless and girlish (although quite adamant that he's *not* going to take you to bed). And, believe me, you'll have him hooked. I promise you, he won't be able to resist you. Never mind if he's angry. Never mind if he's frustrated. Never mind if he thinks that what he got wasn't worth the price of the meal. He got your company, didn't he? And he also got the promise of more. He should be satisfied with that already. Kiss him good night; tell him he's marvelous; and do make a date to see him again.

By the time you've read this book (particularly if you've also read its predecessor) you're going to be a very much more than reasonable lover. You see now why I took you on a detour through the topics of erotic fantasy and orgasmic intercourse and unusual sex before we arrived at what seems like a very much straightforward sexual subject? You're going to know about all of these things even before the boss of your dreams takes you into his bed (or you entice him into yours). So when you *do* say yes, you're going to make his eyes water. He's not just going to be infatuated with you, he's going to love you.

Here's Mary, 25, who set her heart on seducing her boss at the off-Madison Avenue advertising agency where she worked. Mary is the kind of girl who can turn any head in the street: pretty, elegant, with a mass of curly blonde hair and a stunning 38–24–26 figure. "Edgar liked me, liked having me around, liked me being his secretary, but he never once showed that he was interested in me. It was generally understood in the office that he was a devoted family man. He had pictures of his children on his desk, and he always left the office punctually at six-thirty so that he could catch the train back to New Rochelle. He was very handsome, kind of European looking, with fair hair that was just turning gray; very tall, too, the kind of man who makes you feel very small and feminine and petite. I spent months taking care of him, arranging his lunch dates, reminding him when his son's birthday fell due, reminding him to take flowers to his wife, Fenella.

"Then one day I thought to myself, why am I breaking my butt to make him feel happy when *I'm* not happy? I wanted that man, and whatever they say about morals and ethics, I thought I was entitled at least to show him that I wanted him. I mean he wasn't Fenella's property, or anything like that, was he? He was his own man, and if he felt like he wanted to make love to me, that was his own decision. I knew that *I* wanted to make love to *him*. So one day I said, at about six o'clock, do you have to catch the six-thirty train? He looked surprised, and asked me why. I said I had a personal problem, and I wondered if I could discuss it with him, maybe down at the Irish pub that everybody used to go to at lunchtime. He said he could catch a later train, but that since he was going to stay in the city, he might just as well take me to dinner. I could see then that he was looking at me for the first time like a woman, and not as a secretary. The idea that he and I could get something together was definitely dropping into his head, you know, like a dime into a phone booth. Well, we had dinner together at a little French restaurant with pink tablecloths, Les Petites Gourmandes or something like that. I gave him some long story about losing money on stocks, and he was very serious and advised me to call his personal broker.

"After that, we talked about his home and his family, and I told him that I was brought up in Indiana, and I quoted him that poem by James Whitcomb Riley, you know, the Hoosier poet, 'Such a dear little street it is, nestled away,/From the noise of the city and heat of the day.' Well, by then he was totally stuck on me. He said he didn't have to go home that night, he'd already told his wife that he was having an important dinner with a client, and that we could got to the Pierre. The company had a suite at the Pierre. I have to tell you that I very much wanted to go. He was so attractive. Outside of the office, he was even more attractive than he was when I was working with him. But I said that I had to get home. My roommate was sick and I couldn't leave her all evening. Well, that really threw him. I don't think a woman had ever said no to him before, especially a woman who had invited *him* out and who had spent all evening being warm and giving and working very hard to amuse him, as I had. But he accepted it gracefully, he wasn't a boor, and he gave me a taxi ride back to my apartment. He kissed me, and said that he would like to take me out next week. I said, 'We're not getting into anything, are we?' But he said, 'No, I just want to know you better, that's all.'

"Well, I went out with him the following week. I bought myself a new dress, white, very silky and clingy, and I had my hair cut and I plucked my eyebrows and I painted my nails. I waxed my legs, shaved my pubic hair, and made sure that I looked completely stunning. He took me to the Quilted Giraffe, and I didn't realize that he was really showing off because usually you have to make reservations weeks in advance. We had lobster with scallops and the whole evening was perfect. He took me back to the Pierre and we had late-night cocktails; then we went up to our suite. He knew that I was going to say yes, but he still wasn't totally sure. He kissed me, and held me close, and then he undressed me.

It didn't take long. I was only wearing my evening dress and my pantyhose, no underwear. He made love to me very slowly, considering how long I'd kept him waiting. I knew he was very tense, frustrated mostly, but he controlled himself, and he was very graceful and athletic, and that encouraged me to be graceful and athletic too. I raised my hips and opened my thighs as if I were a ballerina, and he poised himself over me and pushed his penis into me all in one long graceful motion. I could look up and see his thick glistening shaft slowly moving up and down, parting the lips of my vagina, and his pubic hair was gray and curly and short, as if he clipped it. And his balls were so tight they could have been crimson walnuts. I didn't have a climax. I wasn't aroused enough, not in that sense. It was more romantic than erotic.

"After it was all over he asked me if I had enjoyed it, and I said yes. We smoked Turkish cigarettes, a very exotic smell. We were lovers for 352 days, I counted them. Then somebody told Fenella, and Fenella made a fuss. She even wrote to the chairman of the company, telling him all about it, and suggesting that he fire me. Well, it was all very nasty, but I think that I had realized right from the very beginning that it would never last. That knowledge gave me the strength to survive it. It seemed to have been such a brief time, from the moment I had first said no to the moment when Edgar said that he couldn't see me anymore. I know now why people who have been married for ten years or more say that their whole married life seems to have passed them by in a flash. In one blink, I was in love with Edgar, and in one blink it was all over. I can remember so much of it.

"One weekend, up at Lake Champlain, it was like heaven, walking along the lakeside, with all the trees reflected. Walking around the city, on cold December evenings with the Santas ringing their bells and the smell of bagels all around. Making love in all kinds of smart hotels, the Plaza, the Algonquin, the Waldorf-Astoria; eating at the Four Seasons; being in love. I think I got the best out of Edgar and also the worst out of him, because I saw him when he was strong and ostentatious, and I also saw him when he was weak and frightened. If you ask me now, I'd say that he would probably have been happier if he'd have left Fenella and come to live with me, in the long run. But in the short run it was too much pain for him to handle, especially since he was right on the verge of promotion. Too much pressure, too much stress. I expect he regrets it now. But love is one thing, and regret is another. Regret doesn't carry any responsibilities."

If you want to keep your boss's sexual attention for as long as possible (and that can include forever), you will have to prove to him that you are better than any other woman he has ever known—including his wife, if he has one. And let's face it, successful businessmen *do* have a very awkward habit of being married, usually to their childhood sweethearts, or worse.

Being better means being a better listener, being more sympathetic, being better in bed (and don't think you've got it all your own way, because in the next chapter I'm going to be telling wives how they can liven up the sexual side of their marriages so that their husbands won't even think of straying). You're going to have to be prepared to give your sexual relationship with your boss everything you've got and make sure that going to bed with you is the most memorable sexual experience of his whole life.

And how do you do that? Here are some hints:

- Fellate him as a natural part of your foreplay.

While you may not be a natural fan of oral sex or feel that you are particularly adept at it, he will certainly appreciate a woman who gives him mouth-to-organ excitement on his first sexual encounter with her.

- Overact a little. There's no harm in it, and if he's really good, you may not have to. As you approach your climax, twist and moan and shake and tell him how fabulous he is. He may not be all that fabulous (remember he is under some pressure), but you can gently educate him later into arousing you the way you really enjoy the best.

- Every two hours or so during your first night together, wake him up and tease him into giving you more. He'll wake up tired the following morning, and so will you, but he will feel like a hell of a guy, and he will think that you are a hell of a woman.

- Continue to be flirtatious with him throughout the following day, giving him big eyes when nobody else in the office is looking. Even if he has to go back to his wife that evening or off to a business meeting, make sure that he knows how much you're looking forward to the next time—and the time after that. Before he leaves you, give him a quick, intimate caress, so that he'll find that breaking up is oh so very hard to do.

Married men, and particularly men who are married to other woman, very often make the very best lovers. But as I have warned you from the beginning, entering into an affair with a man who is wedded to his work, or his wife, or both, is something that has to be done with your eyes wide open. The statistical chances are that you will have the sexual time of your life, but that you'll end up getting hurt.

This is Cynthia, from New York, a 24-year-old secretary in the communications business: "The first time I saw Jim I fell completely in love with him, starry eyes, the whole bit. Then one day he asked me to come to Washington with him to help him make a presentation. And the second night we were there, he took me out to dinner, and afterwards we went to bed together. I knew he was married, but he was so attractive that I didn't feel like resisting. He was a marvelous lover, so assured and attentive and just competent. He was absolutely the best lover I'd ever had, bar none. Well, we continued our affair for two or three months after that, but then somebody at the office called his wife and told her what was going on, and she actually came to the office and told him that it was her or me. I was very fond of him, but I knew what I was going to have to do.

"I quit my job and I never went back there. I thought, if he's really crazy about me, he knows where I live, he'll come after me. If he isn't, then I shouldn't be hanging around making his work and his marriage difficult for him. But, you know, I met him about two years later, and we had a drink together. He said he always had fantastic memories of me, and he really appreciated what I had done. 'I didn't love you,' he said. At least he was honest. But he did say that making love to me had changed his whole view of his life and his marriage and that he had come out of our affair as a much more appreciative person. With a better marriage, too. So don't anyone ever tell me that mistresses aren't good for men, whether they end up marrying them or not."

On the whole, the sexual etiquette of having an affair with a man you work with can be summed up by saying that it is selfish and unfair ever to put him into a position where his career is jeopardized. Be discreet at the office. And even when the affair is over, never tell tales. If you really love him, however, you have every right to fight for him as hard as anyone else, including his wife. Ultimately, the choice of what he does will be his, but you do have your own happiness to consider, and I have never believed that you can condemn anyone for fighting for her own happiness or for the happiness of the one they love. There is little enough of it around, make sure you get your share.

Although you probably *will*, there is no onus on you to feel guilty or responsible for his wife and family. That *cri de coeur* that must go up a thousand times a day all over the world from betrayed wives to new lovers, "Why don't you leave us alone?" is understandable; but there is so much more at stake in human relationships these days than unquestioning loyalty and dogged devotion. In sexual affairs, happiness and communication on both sides are paramount, and if a man has lost both of those qualities in his marriage and seeks them with you, then you are entitled to the rewards that your care and interest in him will bring you, as well as the heartaches, I'm afraid.

All I can say to wives is just make sure that you rate better at everything than the other women in your man's life. Then you'll never lose him.

What happens when you're the boss at the office and you happen to fall for a subordinate man? Being a woman boss, you'll have to be doubly discreet, since there is still a considerable imbalance between what a company and its staff will consider acceptable behavior from a man, and what they will tolerate from a woman. A male boss will often be considered to be nothing more than exercising his *droit du seigneur*, whereas a woman will almost immediately be labeled a nymphomaniac, especially if the man with whom she is having an affair is younger.

The rules are that when you're seeing your member of your staff outside of the office, you should expect him to conduct himself like any man should: opening doors for you, tipping waiters and doormen, and generally treating you like a lady. But you will have a certain edge on him. Trysting times, particularly when they have to be fitted into office hours, will be yours to choose, as will the locations for your loving. You will find that you can use your office authority in non–work-related situations, such as where he's going to take you to dinner and dancing and how frequently you should make love.

This is Agnes, a 34-year-old senior administrator in a Wall Street brokerage firm: "My assistant was truly delicious, a 25-year-old boy straight out of accountancy school, tall, blond-haired, an excellent runner and tennis player. His name was Josh. Well, Josh and I often worked late together. My husband didn't mind me working late at the office because he usually works even later than me. Then one evening, when my husband was in California, and Josh knew that he was in California, he invited me out for dinner. It wasn't expensive. He only earned a quarter of what I did, and so he knew that it was no use trying to impress me. A little Italian place in the Village, just off University. Would you believe that I accepted more because I was hungry than for any other reason? Anyway, we had delicious fettucine, dry white wine, and skewered quails.

"Then he asked me to go back to his apartment with him. It was a small place, but neat, on Tenth Street. There were posters on the walls, it reminded me of all the apartments I'd ever had in New York when I was younger. We talked until late and played music, Bizet, Vivaldi, and then he asked me to come to bed with him. I could see myself in the mirror of his room. I *looked* older than him, and, of course, I was more formally dressed, Gray silk blouse, black skirt, hair cut rather severe. But he undressed me as if he were undressing a young girl, and when he kissed me I closed my eyes and I could almost imagine I was on my first date again. He wasn't particularly stylish in bed, he didn't caress me and stimulate me enough before he got on top of me and started fucking me, but he was very strong, and I was turned on just by his muscles and his sheer athleticism. I could dig my nails into his buttocks and they were as hard as rocks, and his chest and his waist were so trim.

"Later that night, it was my turn. I started to kiss him and stroke him when he was asleep, and gradually he woke up. He was very beautiful to look at, he was like a young god. I took his penis in my hand and massaged it until it was hard; but when he tried to roll over and climb on top of me again, I pushed him gently back. I knelt beside him and fellated him, and do you know what the joy of it was? If I had done this to my husband Paul, he would have wondered what on earth I was doing, whether I'd gone crazy or something, or if I wanted $500 for a new evening gown. But with Josh I could be completely uninhibited. I licked and sucked the head of his penis, and massaged the shaft, and even put his testicles into my mouth, and gently joggled them on my tongue. He was bursting to get on top of me then, but still I wouldn't let him; I made him kiss my breasts and caress me, and lick my clitoris until I was as anxious to have intercourse as he was. That was the difference about making love with somebody who worked for me, and somebody younger, too. I could control the pace of our lovemaking to suit my needs, and believe me it was such a luxury after being with a husband who always made love his way, whether I got any pleasure out of it or not.

"I had a whole series of tremendous orgasms that night, one after the other, until I thought they'd never stop. We made love only four or five times after that, although we often had dinner together or went for walks in the park or down by the river. In the end, he simply said that we shouldn't see each other socially anymore, and I knew he was right. In the end, he went off to join a firm of accountants in Denver, Colorado, although he did send me a photograph of himself skiing at Aspen. Look—here's the picture here. See what he's written on it? 'Thanks, boss—love, Joshua.' Cute, isn't it?"

What did Agnes learn from her relationship? "I think for a woman boss to have an affair with a man who works for her is quite emotionally dangerous and also dangerous careerwise. Men are regarded as studs; women are regarded as hookers. I think it is very inappropriate for a woman to sleep with any man to gain any kind of business advantage; your sex life should not be used as career leverage, otherwise the two sides of your life will be in danger of entanglement. And apart from the emotional stress involved, both can go out of the window at the same time. Whereas if you keep them apart, at least you've still got your job if you lose your lover, and at least you've still got your lover if you lose your job."

Affairs between women bosses and their male subordinates tend on the whole to be short, fierce, and intense. Not many men can live with the situation for long, because once they feel closely attracted to a woman, they want to take over some responsibility for her, both sexual and social; it's a natural instinct. Yet if she's the boss, that natural instinct will be stymied, leading to frustration, resentment, and feelings of inadequacy.

So if you're a woman boss and you have an eye on one of your young hirelings, my advice is to make it discreet, make it burn bright while it lasts, and then grit your teeth and be prepared for a sudden ending.

Agnes: "The beauty of it was for me that for a few short weeks I could indulge my sexual appetite to the utmost, with somebody who was both capable and willing to satisfy me, and over whom I had a very large degree of influence. It was a bit like having a gigolo, only it was better than that, because it was free."

What does a man want out of a perfect affair? He wants sex, obviously; but he wants his sex to be different and startling and romantic. Because of their different approaches to sexual stimulation, it's sometimes easy to forget that most men are just as deeply romantic as women and that they will get a catch in their throat every bit as snarly as yours when they watch a slushy movie like "Brief Encounter" or want to express their love for you.

Be sensitive to his sense of romance. Some women have a disconcerting and destructive habit of sneering at men when they bring them roses or look at them with those celebrated melting eyes, and I would estimate that 73 percent of women have no idea how to accept a compliment gracefully.

Men may often be rude, thoughtless, macho, and insensitive; but when they are showing how much they care about you, make a point of showing them in return how much you appreciate their efforts. I often think that many men become boorish in their attitude toward women simply because all their efforts to be romantic have been met by responses like, "Oh, don't be so ridiculous," or "Roses? They're a bit old-fashioned, aren't they?"

If a man pays you a compliment, learn how to smile and look pleased and accept it. All you have to do is say "Thank you." Practice saying it in the mirror. Pretend that some sincere young guy from the office has just told you that you're beautiful. That's it, lower your head slightly. Smile. Then, "Thank you." That's all it takes.

Never, ever, deny a compliment. If a man tells you you're beautiful, don't say, "Oh, I'm *not*," because what you'll be doing is criticizing his judgment, denigrating his feelings, and making him feel embarrassed for having said it. None of these responses is going to make him think very much better about you. It will also make him hesitate when he feels like complimenting you again.

The same goes for every part of your body, not just your face. If he says, "You've got beautiful breasts," at least try to look as if you're pleased. I've met so many women who snarl whenever a man says anything like that to them in bed, simply because they're embarrassed at being complimented and don't know how to handle their embarrassment except by denying the compliment and sniping back at the poor fellow who paid it to them.

You will hear it time and time again, though. Man says to woman, "I adore you in that dress," and she says, "Oh, it's only an old one." Man says to woman, "You make love beautifully," and she says, "Oh, I'm no good at it at all." Man says to woman, "I love your eyes," and she says, "They're too small."

Don't do it. It's a complete denial of the purpose of a closely communicative sexual relationship. And quite apart from that it's arrogant and rude. When you go to a party or a dinner and you see the women around whom the men cluster the most, they're the women who know they're attractive, whether they're actually beautiful or not, and will accept with pleasure any complimentary remark that they're given.

Learn to pay compliments, too. Men do like to be told that they're looking good when they're dressed up to go out, the same way that women do. They also like to be told that they have enormous penises. This is a sure-fire 100 percent guaranteed compliment, especially when you hold it in your fist and stare at it with a mixture of admiration, anticipation, and trembling anxiety. "I didn't know it was possible for a man to have such a big one," she warbled, breathlessly. (Don't, of course, make the faux pas of saying, "Gosh, this is much bigger than John's dick." When he's making love to you, the last thing he wants to be thinking about is some other man making love to you, either before or later.) After making love, tell him what feelings he gave you; tell him how good he is. Words aren't expensive, but sincere compliments are as valuable as gold.

Be romantic in your affair by grooming yourself well, using exotic perfumes, and cultivating that hint of feminine mystique that many feminists seem to have forgotten about. There is nothing submissive about being alluring. And, sometimes, when he wants to take you out, say no, you're washing your hair or you're spending the afternoon with a girlfriend. Go and do it, too, no matter how much you really feel like seeing him. Wash your hair, play yourself some music, paint your nails, give yourself some breathing space, and make yourself just a little bit hard to get. If he's really aching to see you, he'll come around.

Treat your moments of sex together as celebratory events that happen outside of normal space and time. If you're inviting him back to your apartment, make it comfortable, quiet, warm. So many men, particularly married men, enjoy affairs because they give them a sanctuary, a place and a person away from the pressures of their everyday lives. If you can provide that sanctuary, then you'll be surprised how long your affair lasts and how rewarding it will become. This may sound crass, in this modern world of ours, but it will do you no harm at all to be more poetic in the way you think, more reflective, more romantic in the sense that you are intensely aware of your surroundings and intensely aware of your lover, too, even his heartbeat.

Carole, 28, from Baltimore, said, "I love affairs that are a little bit unreal, like the movies. Favorite restaurants, walks through the park. Because you're infatuated, because you're in love, you become conscious of how romantic you are, and how good you look with the wind in your hair, standing by the seashore with thunderheads piling up in the distance. I don't think there's anything wrong in it; it's exciting and pleasing and good for you. I've had two beautiful affairs, really beautiful, and both men still write to me and say what a good time they had. I made those affairs good, like a vacation, or a happy dream, and every part of them was wonderful, from the dancing to the arguing to the lovemaking. Even the end was good, when we said goodbye. We played it out like the end of 'Casablanca,' or 'Elvira Madigan,' or something like that. The hurt was real, just like the pleasure had been real, but just because something hurts, that's no reason why it can't be beautiful."

13

How to Be the Most Exciting Woman Your Husband Will Ever Know

Sex is a physical and emotional thrill, and like all thrills, if you experience it often enough, it will lose its excitement and become routine. That is why the sex lives of many married couples, over the years, become less and less stimulating, less and less creative, and less and less important in relation to all the other elements that concern them, like their house, and their children, and their financial problems.

The danger, of course, lies in the fact that even in late middle-age you are still capable of intense and deeply rewarding sexual experiences, and just because you and your husband are no longer arousing each other as much as you used to, that doesn't mean that somebody else couldn't arouse you to those onetime heights of ecstasy—or that somebody else couldn't turn your husbnad on the way that *you* used to.

Maggie, 38, a housewife, told me, "I suppose we have sex once or twice every week. Sometimes it's quite good, sometimes it doesn't amount to very much. Jack was always a gentle lover, always quiet. Sometimes, after we've made love, I lie there and wonder what sex is all about, why everybody makes such a fuss about it."

There are hundreds and thousands of middle-aged wives and lovers like Maggie; wives and lovers who have almost forgotten what it was about sex that used to arouse them so much. Most of them will go through the rest of their married lives without ever having the opportunity to remember; many will go through the personal tragedy of losing their husbands to women who have learned that a dull and routine sex life isn't always the husband's fault alone and that they can easily steal away another woman's man if only they show him what he's been missing.

You deserve much more than a routine sex life. You deserve excitement, arousal, and constant satisfaction. But you will never get it by feeling sorry for yourself and lying back and waiting for your husband or lover to wake up to the fact that he ought to be making love to you better. Whether the dullness of your sex life is your fault or not, you will have to make a positive effort to stir up that man in your life and do for him what another woman would do is she were out to excite him.

Your state of mind as you approach the problem of a routine sex life is very important. No matter how much you feel that your husband's sex technique ought to be better, no matter how much you feel that *he* ought to be making all the effort, that *he* should be wooing you instead of the other way around, just remember that two wrongs don't make a right and that two indifferent people can't even start to reconstruct their sex life. So think positively, and don't lay any blame, even when you get embarrassed, even when you get angry. The minute you start laying blame, you start laying up resentment, and it is a combination of resentment and lack of caring that drives so many couples away from each other. Promise yourself that you're going to be sexy, forgiving, provocative, and infinitely patient. You will get your reward in seventh heaven.

Once you have decided that you want to do something to improve your sex life and that you can tackle it without feeling furious about your husband's slow responses, then you are ready to start. And why not start today, because there is no better time to begin to give yourself the sexiest time of your life than right now, as soon as you possibly can.

Take a good long critical look at yourself in the mirror. Your appearance, your grooming, your weight, your hair, your clothes. Are you as smart and as slim and as attractive as you think your husband would like you to be? Or have you allowed yourself to go to seed just a little? Just a little, maybe? Don't wash your hair as often as you ought to? Don't varnish your nails? Don't have that bright get-up-and-go-to-bed look that used to turn him on so much?

If you feel you have any shortcomings when you look in the mirror, you know what to do about them. Buy yourself some fresh makeup, some fresh perfume, and perk yourself up. Consider changing your hairstyle; not only so that *he* will suddenly have to look at you with fresh eyes, but so that *you* will feel differently, too. It's important for you to feel refreshed and renewed, as if you've left the old dull you behind and started a new, sexier, brighter life.

Take a look at your wardrobe. How attractive and modern are your clothes? If you're tired of them, then *he's* going to be tired of them, too, and it's surprising how often a new item of clothing as simple and cheap as a T-shirt can buck up your husband's interest in you.

Now look at your grooming—your nails and your hands and your skin. Have you been looking after yourself as well as you ought to? Have you waxed your legs lately? Shaved under your arms? Shave off your pubic hair—that will change your appearance as well as arouse him and will also give you the feeling that you're really doing something positively erotic.

Think about what you're going to be doing. You're going to be sexier, less inhibited; you're going to start experimenting with sex and you're going to do everything you can to drive your husband completely wild in bed, not just tonight but every night. You're going to have sex not just once a week, not just twice a week, but six or seven times a week, sometimes more. And if any of this newly ignited sexuality startles your husband, all you have to tell him is that this was the kind of sex you always wanted only you were too shy to ask until now. And show him this book, if you want to. Then he'll understand.

Buy yourself some new sexy underwear. Start to make a point of *not* wearing underwear at all unless it's really necessary; you'll be surprised how quickly you get out of the habit and prefer the freer feeling of walking around naked under your dresses. Think to yourself: Nothing, but *nothing*, is going to make me feel sexually embarrassed. I'm a grown-up, independent, sexually liberated lady, and if I feel like dressing and behaving like this, then I'm going to.

Get to know yourself sexually. Read the chapters on exploring your sexual anatomy, and spend some time at home on your own, stimulating yourself with your fingers or with a vibrator, learning how best to arouse yourself so that you can show your husband *exactly* how to touch you to excite you the most. Masturbate yourself to orgasm over and over; it's your body, and you're retraining it, so you can do whatever you like without embarrassment and without inhibition.

Prepare yourself for some of the more adventurous sexual diversions by probing your bottom with your vibrator (making sure, of course, that it's liberally lubricated and that you don't let go of the end of it). You can use a candle for this if you prefer, or a cucumber, or anything that has a phallic shape. Get used to the muscular actions you have to make in order to admit an erection into your anus.

Consider trying some of the sex stars' favorite tricks, such as deep-throat technique that made Linda Lovelace notorious. Actually, deep-throating was not invented by the redoubtable Ms. Lovelace but was an advanced variation of fellatio originally practiced by the leading geishas of Japan. It involves taking a man's penis not just into your mouth but all the way down your throat, until it can penetrate no further. It does take some practice; first, you have to teach yourself to repress your natural instinct to gag whenever anything is thrust down the back of your throat. This reflex can be gradually overcome by regularly putting your finger into the back of your throat, until you can touch yourself there without having an urge to gag. When you deep-throat your husband, your head should be stretched back like a sword swallower's, so the best position is probably lying on the bed on your back with you head hanging over the edge. Your husband can then kneel on the floor in front of you and carefully slide his erection into your mouth. It takes time and patience to learn to do it really well, but what do you have in your marriage except time and patience? Make up your mind that you're going to do it, and do it really erotically, and keep on urging your husband to try and try again.

Sandra, a 32-year-old receptionist from Seattle, taught herself to deep-throat after going to see the movie. "I was knocked out by it. I thought it was so erotic. I was sure that if they could do it in the film, then I could do it, too. One Saturday evening, after we'd come home from dinner with friends and Roger was getting ready to go to bed, I lay back on the cover and said, 'Let's try it, you know, the deep-throat thing.' Believe it or not, he didn't want to at first. Our sex life hadn't been very sparkling for quite a long time, and I think he was shy or embarrassed. But when he came over to kiss me, I reached up into his robe, and held on to his cock, and rubbed it two or three times until it started to rise up. And I said, 'Come on, let's try it, I want to.' So he kissed me some more, and then he knelt down, and I put my head back and started to suck him and rub him until he was incredibly hard.

"At last I guided him in deeper, and his whole cock filled up my mouth. I thought that I was going to choke or that I wasn't going to be able to breathe, but Roger took his cock out a little way, and I realized that I could breathe in between thrusts. I reached around and took hold of his hand, and tugged on it to show him that I wanted him actually to fuck me in my mouth, not like sucking, and that's what he did. It was incredible; I'd never had any experience like it. I wanted it to go on and on, this huge cock sliding right in and out of my mouth and my throat. But he came very quickly, and he shot the whole lot straight down my throat, I swallowed it without even tasting it. We still do it now and then, not very often, because I have to be in the mood for it. But he's proud because he's got a wife who can deep-throat, and that's enough for me."

Marilyn Chambers, star of "Behind the Green Door," was another star whose oral sex technique was quite spectacular. Blue movie critic Bill Rotsler described how she had once fellated a friend at a party. "Kneeling naked between Johnnie's legs,

Marilyn demonstrated a fellatio technique that was very erotic to watch. At each suck his body undulated, and it was as if the 'suck' rippled slowly and sensuously throughout her entire beautiful body. If it was 'acting' it was superb acting: if it was real, my congratulations to her lovers. In either case, it was beautiful, subtle, and erotic."

An erotic technique recommended by several sex stars and several well-qualified ladies of pleasure (including that warm and fun-loving Xaviera Hollander) is the *direct* massage of your husband's prostate gland during intercourse. You'll recall from my chapter on the male anatomy (and you're welcome to flip back to it if you don't) that the prostate gland is where the two vas deferentia join together and where much of the fluid that composes semen is produced. Although it is way up inside your husband's groin, slightly below and behind his pubic bone, it can be stimulated by inserting your finger into his anus, straight upward until your finger can't go in any further, and then massaging the wall of his rectum with your fingertip. Of course, if he is really relaxed, and you moisten your fingers first with juice from your vagina, you may be able to insert two or even three fingers into his anus and give him a full internal massage. The sensation— especially as he approaches his climax—can be dynamic and can give him a deep tremble of pleasure.

It is this kind of passionate and whole-hearted approach to sex that you can use to fire your man up again—kissing him and caressing him every time as if you *urgently* want to make love to him, showing him that you think he's good-looking and sexy and that he arouses you. Sexual arousal is catching, and if you show your husband that you're turned on, and that it's *him* who turns you on, even if you're acting just a little to begin with, he should very quickly respond.

Share your fantasies with him; start talking about

your desires and what you want out of your sex life. If you think that you haven't been making love often enough lately, tell him. There is nothing more destructive in a sexual relationship than silent resentment. After a while, that resentment begins to make it almost impossible for a couple to have carefree, creative sex together. There's always a feeling that "Oh, you may feel like it tonight, but what about tomorrow?"

Remember what I said earlier in this book, that not every act of love has to be amazing. You can't make the earth move every single time, nor should you try. The most ecstatic moments of sex will happen spontaneously, just when you're least expecting them. But to have those ecstatic moments, you've got to be enjoying sex on a regular basis; you can't have peaks without valleys. It's my belief that you should actually overindulge yourself, over and above your normal appetites. You'd be surprised what effect it has on your libido—because the more you have the more you want, and the more you have the more likely you are to experience those peaks of really astonishing pleasure, and the more often you'll be driving your man wild in bed.

So you don't feel like intercourse tonight? Try simply holding your husband while he's sitting up reading in bed and gently caressing his nipples and his penis. The caresses may not lead to anything but a warm goodnight kiss, but there's certainly no harm in that. Every shared act of affection will bind him closer to you and make him realize the benefits of being married to a woman who is strong, positive, and has an active and passionate attitude toward sex.

Ask him one day if there's anything he's ever wanted to do in bed but never quite gotten around to asking you. He may not tell you the first time, but keep on asking him regularly from time to time. If he does have a particular fantasy that he's been keeping hidden from you, you'll discover it sooner or later. Even if you don't want to act it out with him, you could at least talk about it with him while you're making love and coax him into telling you every lurid and erotic detail.

Jenny, a 34-year-old sales assistant from Albany, New York, found that her husband of nine years had always had an extremely vivid fantasy about running a college for professional whores. "He took so long to tell me about it, but in the end he came out with it, bit by bit. It was a very far-out fantasy, but he said he only had it when he was very highly aroused. He said it was a kind of an extension of a book he read called *The Harrad Experiment*, about a college where boys and girls were allowed to share rooms together. Only *this* fantasy revolved around a college where girls were sent at the age of about 18 to train to be high-class hookers. He said they had to be nude all the time, except for stockings and garter belts and shoes, and that all their lessons were about sex, how to make it with men. Their teachers were fantastic looking women with statuesque figures, and they would demonstrate to the girls how to make love, using two or three real men.

"Oh, there was a whole lot more to it, and he said that when he was really excited, the fantasy got incredibly dirty. But instead of just saying *umm*, or telling him that the fantasy was crude, I joined in with it. And although we didn't act it out or anything like that, we used to talk about it together and I'd add little bits to it that turned *me* on, so in the end we had this kind of joint fantasy we could talk about together. I added this bit where they had a sort of a sports day, you know, all these naked girls, and they were climbing ropes and getting really turned on, and doing all these athletic exercises naked. I know it sounds odd when you talk about it flat like this—when you're not turned on; but it's amazing how sexy it can make you feel when you're talking about it with your husband, in bed. I was terrifically aroused by one scene he described in which one girl has to satisfy six men at once, for a sort of sexual exam. She has two penises crammed into her mouth at one time, she's holding one penis in each hand, she has one man behind her, making love to her anally, and another man making love to her vaginally. If she's really good, she can make them all climax together, and then there are showers of semen everywhere. I don't know, that just turned me on. I guess I could imagine myself as the girl."

Jenny demonstrated that erotic fantasies can be closely shared between couples, especially when they have lived and made love together long enough to trust each other implicitly.

Sharing your desires and expressing your needs, even to someone you love, can take considerable courage. You may find when you first start confessing your urges to your husband that he doesn't respond in kind. But if instead of feeling embarrassed or out on a limb you take things easy, step by step—if you have confidence in your own sexuality and your ability to be able to arouse him—then you'll find after a while that he gains the confidence to be able to confide *his* desires in *you*.

"It took my husband eleven years to pluck up the courage to tell me that he wanted to see me with my pussy shaved," said 37-year-old Florence, from Charleston, South Carolina. "It took me about eleven minutes to do what he wanted."

Florence blamed herself afterward for not realizing that some little something had been buzzing around in her husband's head for so long. If she had been more forthcoming, more active in her sex life, then she would have. Mind you, I think her husband was more than a little on the slow side about expressing his erotic preferences.

You should *think* about your sex life with your husband. After all, you lavish an extraordinary amount of thought and planning on the special meals you cook for him. (Why shouldn't you lavish just as much attention on making love to him? Make an evening of sex different and exciting in some way. It doesn't have to be much. It doesn't have to be anything more than greeting him at the door and telling him you're not wearing any panties. Of course, it can be as blatantly sexual as dressing up in a rubber mask and shiny rubber thigh boots and inviting him to go down on you or else.

And sexual moments don't have to be confined to the bedroom or even to the living room carpet. When was the last time you slid your hand into his pants and masturbated him as he drove along the freeway? When was the last time you took a bath with him? When was the last time you had sex up against a tree in the woods? It doesn't take very much imagination, all it takes is sexual initiative, and the understanding that these days, being the independent woman you are, you don't have to wait for your husband to make the first move.

Of course, you're a woman, and that means that you don't always want to be setting the pace of your sexual relationship with your husband. And some husbands, let's be honest, resent being told what to do or even being gently shown what to do. You will have to make your own judgment on your husband's tolerance to your born-again sexual friskiness. It's important that he doesn't feel that you're disappointed with him or that you're somehow criticizing his virility or his sex drive. To my mind, one of the best ways of overcoming this sensitive problem is to show him your copy of this book—and explain to him that you're simply doing everything you can to increase the sexual excitement in your marriage for both of you.

If you don't think he'll take too kindly to that, be more subtle in your sexual approaches to him. Concentrate on the romantic side of your relationship as much as the erotic side. Tell him you love him. Tell him, in fact, that you think you've fallen in love with him all over again. Tell him you saw him outside in the yard yesterday and you thought what a good-looking man he was. Kiss him, tell him you love him; and that night, when you're in bed together, tell him again, and beg him to make love to you. That way, if he's one of those men who prefers to think that they're always in control, you'll begin to win him over to your new and sexually active way of life without making him feel that he was in any way inadequate. Feelings of inadequacy (however deserved they sometimes may be) are not to be encouraged in husbands and lovers. They do very little to promote good lovemaking, and they play havoc with a man's hardness.

Ten years after *How to Drive Your Man Wild in Bed*, I see this book as an ongoing encouragement to all of those fantastic and enthusiastic women like you who take a serious interest in pleasing their men and pleasing themselves. I have kept all of your letters over the years, and they have formed the basis of what I hope has been an up-to-date and constructive guide for future pleasures. If you want to write and share your own experiences, please do so, so that in another few years we can talk again about even *more* ways to drive your man wild in bed.

Let's close this chapter now with some words from Veronica, a 29-year-old photographer's assistant from Cambridge, Massachusetts, who wrote me after reading *How to Drive Your Man Wild in Bed*, "Women regard men as stereotypes just as

much as men regard women as sexual stereotypes, and most of the time they're completely
wrong. Men have incredible sexual sensitivity, a
deep-rooted anxiety about sexual failure, and a des-
perate need to prove themselves to the women they
love and the women that attract them. All the men
that I've ever known have been like that, anyway,
and I've known dozens. The brash macho ones are
just as afraid of sexual failure as the shy retiring
ones; their brashness is a way of hiding their anxiety, that's all. I've read this book now, and apart
from all the sexual tricks and techniques, I think
the most important and valuable thing it shows is
that women are equal and positive partners in sexual relationships, or at least they ought to be. In
some cases, they are in a better position to improve
the quality of the relationship than the man is. I believe it's time we stopped being sexually afraid of
men, because there really is nothing to fear. The
way ahead to really fantastic sex lies in just what
you've said—in communication between the sexes,
in men and women at last admitting to each other
that they're on the same side. Be sexier, that's my
motto. And there are no mottoes more rewarding
than that."

For that written opinion, Veronica gets a bottle of
champagne and an invitation to come back in ten
years time and give me another opinion on the next
book.

14
Fifty Sexy Things You Can Do for Your Man

Some of the tips and techniques in this chapter have already been discussed in the preceding chapters, but I thought it worthwhile to give you an erotic shopping list to make it easier for you to decide how you're going to turn him on today.

You can go through the whole list of 50 in numerical order, or you can dodge around, but make sure that you cross each item off as you do it. And write your opinion of both his and your reactions next to it. It doesn't have to be a long report; "Mmmm" or "ouch" would be enough.

1. Greet him at the door with no panties on, and *tell* him you don't have any panties on.
2. Greet him at the door with nothing on but stockings and a garter belt.
3. Don't greet him at the door at all, but make sure that you're waiting for him upstairs in bed, stark naked. And don't spoil it by hiding under the covers.
4. Open his pants while he's watching a baseball game and start to masturbate him.
5. Slide your hand into your jeans while you're

both watching "Dynasty" and start to masturbate yourself.

6. After dinner, sit next to him on the couch and start to kiss his cock.
7. Suggest you take a shower together, for a change. And take it. And make sure that you soap him all over. And that he soaps *you* all over.
8. Fellate him in the shower.
9. Fellate him in bed. Do it slowly, take your time, relish it.
10. Demand that he licks you until you reach an orgasm.
11. Sit on his face and order him to lick you to orgasm.
12. Ask him the sexiest thing he's ever thought of.
13. Ask him if he's ever wanted to do something really erotic and hasn't wanted to tell you what it is.
14. Make him lie on his back on the bed, and make love to him.
15. Bite his nipples.
16. Tell him to take you for a drive in the car someplace, with you wearing only a trench coat and nothing else.
17. Ask him to park someplace private and make love to you in the back seat.
18. Go out naked into the garden with him at nighttime and make love on the grass, in the flowerbeds, under the trees, anywhere.
19. Ask him to masturbate for you and to ejaculate over your bare breasts.
20. Masturbate in front of him, and show him just how you like to be caressed.
21. Make love to him with a buzzing vibrator up inside your bottom.
22. Do the same for him. Twist it around and

around, as if you're stirring a pudding (but make sure that you don't let go).

23. Ask him to make love to you anally, but make sure he takes care not to hurt you.

24. Dress up for him like a San Francisco whore, with wasp-waisted basque and a feather hat.

25. Talk very dirty to him. Use all the crudest words you know. Insist that he fucks you, and that he fucks you hard.

26. Hurt him while he makes love to you. Dig your nails into his buttocks and bite his shoulder muscles. Claw at his anus with your sharp fingernails. But go gently with the testes.

27. Insist that he makes love to you while *he* is naked and *you* are completely dressed.

28. Suggest that he tie you hand and foot to the bed with scarves, and do to you whatever he wants, for as long as he wants. (Reminder: Don't do this with a man you don't completely trust.)

29. Spank him and rub his penis at the same time.

30. Next time you're out in company with him, come across and whisper in his ear that you'd love to kiss his cock.

31. Next time you're out in company, drag him into the bedroom or bathroom, and thrust his hand up between your legs.

32. Tell him you love him, and kiss him very slowly and seductively.

33. Hold his cock for him while he pees. If you're outside and it's been snowing, you can write your name.

34. Fellate him until he reaches a climax, and then make a greedy show of sucking and swallowing his semen.

35. Hold him and caress him in bed, kiss his

neck and his back, gently stroke him, and tell him he's beautiful.

36. Start fellating him when he's asleep.

37. Tie his wrists and his ankles up with leather bondage straps, and do whatever you want to with him, for as long as you want.

38. When you're out walking or picnicking, masturbate him with your hand, then ask him to shoot his ejaculate into your stretched-open panties so that you'll have to spend the rest of the day with his semen between your thighs.

39. Insist that he goes out to a formal dinner without any underpants on.

40. Challenge him to make you reach a climax just by caressing your breasts.

41. Let him take a video of you stripping and stroking yourself in front of the camera.

42. Let him watch you pee, stretching your lips apart with your fingers so that he can see everything.

43. Describe a really private sexual fantasy to him.

44. Call him at work and tell him that you're aching for him, and that you're slowly working yourself up thinking about making love to him, and that your dress is pulled up, and your hand is slowly massaging your vulva, and that you'd do anything to have his cock inside you right at this moment . . .

45. Shave off all of his pubic hair, then massage his bare penis with baby oil, using the Masters and Johnson grip to retard his climax until he can't hold it back any longer. Explosion!

46. Wear high-heeled shoes in bed.

47. Write him a letter when you're away, de-

scribing all the things you'd like him to do to
you if he were with you.

48. Think of the most vulgar, the most sexy, the
most dirty thing you can think of—something
that makes you tremble even to think
about it—and then dare yourself to do it with
him.

49. Tell him you love him.

50. Whatever he's doing right now—right now—
even before you've finished this book—tell
him to make love to you.

You will probably have sexual games of your own
that you will want to add to this list of fifty. You will
have realized by now that they *are* games, that
they're to be played for pleasure only, and that even
those suggestions that contain aspects of so-called
"kinky" sex are harmless and fun and are only
meant to bring out into the open the sadistic and
masochistic side of your sexual drive that everybody
has to a greater or lesser extent and about
which you should never be ashamed. They are part
of what makes sex exciting, part of the erotic power
play between you and your man.

All you have to do now is go out and enjoy yourself
with the man you love. There's very little more
for me to say except thank you for reading; thank
you for being the new kind of woman who has made
the 1980's a very much more lively and exciting decade
to live in—and make sure you drive that man
of yours really wild, or I'll want to know why.

About the Autho

GRAHAM MASTERTON, is the author of two of th most successful manuals of sexual love of all time— *How to Be the Perfect Lover* and *How to Drive You Man Wild in Bed*.

He is the former editor of *Penthouse* and *Forum* magazines and has written nine books on sexua subjects, including two classic works on erotic dreams. He is married and has three sons.